MEMOS TO DAN

Entrepreneurial Lessons from a Father to his Son

By
Todd W. Stetson
& Lynn W. Stetson

memostodan.com

Library of Congress Control Number: 2018902502
ISBN 13: 978-1-7320648-0-5
ISBN 10: 1-7320648-0-6

10 9 8 7 6 5 4 3 2 1

DEDICATION

For my father-in-law, John.

....

*John built the foundation of a small family business
that is now entering its third generation.*

....

*John, Alzheimers may have stolen your memory,
but you lived your life providing wonderful memories
to your family and friends.*

–Todd

A portion of the proceeds from the sales of these books
will be donated to the Alzheimer's Association (www.alz.org)

Memos to Dan

"This book is different from any other business, managerial or leadership book I've read (in the last 30 years?). While other business books detail useful and practical business concepts, impart wisdom, or summarize leadership qualities of well known, successful Fortune 500 CEOs, **Memos to Dan** embodies the human element of being a successful, ethical business owner, whether big or small. In easy-to-read, quick-hit, impactful 'memos', the reader has a genuine, tangible feel for the challenges and rigor, the sweat and the struggle...and the unbelievably satisfying rewards that come with being a successful owner of a small, family business. This is an enjoyable and captivating read that would be insightful for any young professional considering a career in business, finance or entrepreneurship. **Memos to Dan** artfully demonstrates that true leadership, and success as a small business owner, is also about who you are and not just what you do—that guidance, humility, intelligence, common sense, and compassion, need to be practiced each and every day to achieve desired results."

—Kevin R. Lawler, Venture Capital/Angel Investor

"An essential read for anyone launching or running a small business. Having left the corporate world three years ago to launch a business, I found each of the memos to be filled with insights and nuggets of wisdom. I only wish that I would have read it before I founded my business."

—Mark D. Linsz, co-founder, My Next Season
former Treasurer, Bank of America Corporation

"**Memos to Dan** is at once a professional and personal account of how to successfully launch and run a small business. It offers advice and wisdom to would-be entrepreneurs and to those who are launching and growing a business. The authors write insightfully within a set of 50 brief and easy-to read memos, offering a host of stories and examples on what you need to know and navigate on this journey. From crafting your vision and strategy, to building your team, to managing the finances and having a life outside your business, and much more—to those who are starting, running and growing a business, make sure you get the memos!"

—**Lisa Gundry, Ph.D., DePaul University**
  Department of Management & Entrepreneurship

"**Memos to Dan** is a very practical book—and its practical parts, I must say, are truly excellent. Entrepreneurship is hard to teach effectively because every entrepreneurial venture is patently unique. However, **Memos to Dan** balances specific examples with a solid conceptual foundation to make its lessons highly generalizable. The sections on family business are fascinating— especially when it comes to how and when to navigate the often complicated transitions of a company among family members. The information about mentors is extremely novel—I had never thought about engaging vendors as advisors, but now I will utilize this notion in my own lectures and consulting work. The book's organization is fantastic—it includes a large number of short and specific chapters that make for a very useful handbook."

—**Patrick J. Murphy, PhD, Professor of Entrepreneurship**
  DePaul University

Table of Contents

File #1

Introduction

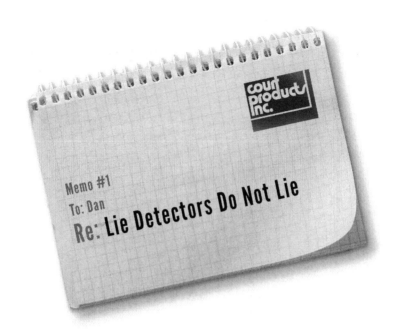

Memo #1
To: Dan
Re: Lie Detectors Do Not Lie

WAS LAYING ON MY BED watching the 1982 World Series between the St. Louis Cardinals and the Milwaukee Brewers in an extended stay hotel off Interstate 40 in Gallup, New Mexico. Outside my door, I heard the unmistakable roar of the rental truck I had driven down from Denver. Realizing that truck held all my worldly possessions including the sum total of my furniture—my waterbed frame and whiskey barrel stereo cabinet, both fashioned with my own hands—and my stereo, I leapt up and ran outside in hot pursuit of my entire net worth.

I frantically sprinted after the truck waving my arms and boldly yelling for the thief to stop. He did—thankfully signaling I was not a victim of an in-process robbery. The driver proceeded to inform me that there had been no payment on the rental and it was past its anticipated return date so he was there to reclaim it. Turns out, the "repo man" was dropped off so I had to drive him back to the rental office. There, I explained I hadn't found any suitable housing yet in Gallup and my hotel room just didn't have the space for my personal treasure trove. Likewise, my employer just told me to keep everything in the rental truck until I sorted out my housing. It was on me that I hadn't let the rental agency know that an extended stay hotel was actually making this newly minted college grad feel like he had all he needed—bed, shower, mini-fridge, TV!

Possessions rescued, I went into work one day during my second week on the job as a Manager Trainee at the local K-Mart. When I arrived, the Manager informed me the store had been robbed and that I would have to take a lie detector test. I think I started to sweat right away. Lie detector tests only happened on TV shows as far as I knew and I also recalled some people failed just because they were nervous about being questioned. I felt for sure that was going to be me.

K-Mart was my first professional gig. I had literally only worked as a lifeguard during all those prior summers. I was admittedly short on experience, but I had a great tan. So here I was, sitting at a table in a bland conference room, lie detector kit spread out in full view and listening to a couple of talking heads about how this interrogation would proceed. To my initial mental flash, it was just like TV—they hook you up to a monitor and asked a few simple questions, it wasn't a very long "interview" at all. There were three of us in the room— me, one guy asking the questions, and one guy watching, probably counting the sweat drops on my forehead. Sitting there, even though you know you are totally innocent, it was quite unnerving. My inner-detective gave me the impression they may have already had an idea who they suspected. Getting a few others in the interrogation mix, however, might allow them to demonstrate how the culprit's test differed—and presumably failed.

I think back to that experience and it is still a horrible way to introduce a new employee to your firm by subjecting them to such a test just as a "control group." How times have changed, I can't imagine anyone getting away with that today, even in "big corporate" America. Today, the entire suspect lineup would have to have the chance to speak to their attorneys beforehand and afforded the choice to opt out. In the end, though, I passed and the truth won out—no surprise to me, of course.

To understate the obvious, this was a real eye-opener and one heck-uva start to the real world of business where my dress code was now a decidedly different kind of suit than my previous summer gigs. That interrogation completed, I promptly provided my two week notice that I would be departing this impersonal, large corporate experiment.

Memo #2
To: Dan
Re: Overview and Preview

SO, YOU ASK, WHERE DID I LAND and why am I writing these memos to Dan. This book is about sharing my journey from indecision about pursuing a college education to becoming a cog in a large corporation to landing in a small business environment to eventually loving, and thriving within, my own small business enterprise.

Who exactly is Dan and why does he need these memos? Well, Dan is my son and he joined me in my small business in 2010 upon graduation from college. One day I will step away from my business and I thought I should provide him with the benefit of my experiences (both good and bad) at starting and running the show. My hope is that as one with an interest in running an entrepreneurial organization, you too can enjoy some of those same benefits from these memos.

This book is not about a rags-to-riches success story nor the latest high tech experiment born in a garage. There is no international espionage or things that explode. Come to think of it, we did have our computer system ransomed for bitcoin by international hackers and a neighboring business' propane tanks did explode forcing us into an emergency evacuation of our industrial park. But, I digress. If this book is one day raised in conversation for having passed on some helpful thoughts and considerations, I'll take that as a great success!

No book, this one included, can pretend to answer (or address) all the questions you need to think about to definitively resolve your career exploration questions. Don't despair, however, take comfort in the knowledge that it is you that has those answers! Through my own experiences, I'll relay my story and my career thoughts with the aim of having you draw parallels, thus enabling you to think through aspects of your own situation and preferences.

It is important to establish a definition of "small business." The term is thrown around quite easily and certainly means different things to different people. As you read through this book, consider a small business not defined by the number of people working in it, per se, rather a business run by a president who also happens to essentially be vice-president of all the other functions. In other words, there are really no organizational "layers" in small business as defined in this book. That said, consider a team of "cashiers" manning the registers within a franchise business supervised by a shift manager. Collectively, the cashiers can be viewed as "one" given the common role. Thus, I wouldn't disqualify using the definition of small business in this one-layer organization. When you start to create multiple departments within a company, you are starting to get into a bigger operation, or a medium sized business.

You will need to explore your potential "fit" within the small business environment and where your personality and interests can be most successful. It takes time to adequately explore these interests, don't expect the first job opportunity to be the answer to all your dreams. Maybe these stories will help you find that quicker, but in any case, it is important to enjoy the journey and keep learning at every stop along the way.

I hope to provide you the benefit of how I engineered some of my successes—and learned from my failures. The stories should reso-nate with students just contemplating a start-up career, those newly initiated entrepreneurs and even the seasoned small business exec-utive. In a small business setting, you quickly find that you won't be able to readily look around to answer the question "how did I do this last time" because there may not have been a "last time." This book may provide you my "last time" experiences from which you can learn.

This book is not designed to be an exhaustive "how to" technical process manual about starting and running your own business. You might find, however, that learning about some of the bumps in my road could be helpful as you drive along your own route to exploring whether working in, or owning, a small business is the right fit for you.

For the younger audience still seeking out their path in the working world, I'd like to help frame your mindset about what might be best for you. We'll explore the questions you should be asking or contemplating. Working in small business will certainly guarantee an overall immersion into all aspects of running a company. Contrast this with a typical first assignment within a large company which tends to operate by creating large numbers of subject matter experts within multiple departments spread across a vast bureaucracy.

I have written this book from the perspective of what I have learned over the past 30+ years working in, and eventually owning, my own small business enterprise. My challenge was, however, I didn't consider myself a writer. Enter my brother, Lynn, who offered to organize and write the book following his own 30+ year career in financial services risk management.

To provide a common thread throughout the book, I openly discuss my company, Court Products, Inc. I lay out these real experiences and my reflections in rich detail, setting this book apart from other collections of unrelated third party stories. The early memos have a bit more background to provide overall context for later topics. Probably much like you, the journey to the doorstep of your interest in small business wasn't exactly (or won't be) a straight line. Importantly, however, the journey will likely reveal some of the key interests, motivations and even frustrations that you will encounter while exploring a small business career.

My business, Court Products, focuses on a service-based model to distribute a range of custom apparel and fitness equipment products to national not-for-profit clubs and organizations. As mentioned, it's not the latest "App" (shame, I might then be a billionaire), but it does share the fundamental requirement that successfully executing basic core business principles and practices is a key to success—that is akin to virtually any other type of business, big or small. The following memos should be able to provide broad-based guidance to address the myriad of questions and situations that arise when running, or working in, a small business.

There are 50 memos in all, plus my "*Afterword.*" The memo style allows you the opportunity to read and think through a couple of complete topics at a time. Further, "Key Takeaways" summarize the critical points at the end of each memo to make it easier for later reference. To provide organization, I've sorted the memos into an introduction and eight additional file folders which align to the high-level issues and considerations of a small business. Each memo addresses an important topic in my company's evolution as well as my development as a business owner. Here is a high-level overview to the organization and progression of this book:

File #2—Is Small Business Right for You?—essentially helps you evaluate whether a career pursuit in small business is a fit from a personality, interests and skills perspective. Your experiences, like mine, may also play deciding roles in influencing this career path. An honest self-assessment of both your personal preferences and your inherent skillset is the right first step before over-committing your intellectual and financial capital to your entrepreneurial effort.

File #3—Getting Started—includes guidance on what type of business makes sense in light of how you articulate your personal profile. It also discusses basic approaches for due diligence you should conduct to evaluate the choice of business you ultimately pursue.

File #4—Setting the Vision and Maintaining a Strategy—discusses the importance of creating a vision for what you want your business to become and how to maintain focus over the long haul, particularly through the challenging early years. A vision is an idealistic, yet attainable, identity for your business. To attain that vision, establishing an effective strategy that maps out the critical initiatives and activities your company must execute is a must. Strategies may evolve over time as dictated by the business environment, but they must ultimately continue to strive toward attaining your vision in order to achieve business success.

File #5—Running the Business Operations—offers up some practical thoughts around how to orient your day-to-day running of the company. What is the best way to focus your attention? On what and for how long? While industry and company dependent, these memos reinforce the undeniable fact that you are the driver of your company's own operational processes and success. As you run the operations, maintaining an understanding of your customers' motivations is key.

File #6—CEO of HR (Every Day!)—addresses a multitude of considerations concerning the team you will assemble and the equally significant number of personnel issues you will be faced with managing over the years. Protecting yourself and building and retaining a talented team requires a great deal of a small business owner's time and attention. There will, of course, be some difficult situations to face, it is almost inevitable over the course of any company's lifespan.

File #7—Chief Administrative Officer—moves beyond the operations and personnel front to the full range of administrative matters that any small business owner must address. From accounting and legal matters to banking and technology, the calendar is always full. Add to this, the potential to reach outside the company to seasoned advisors for some outside perspective to challenge your own thought processes over time.

File #8—& Son (or Daughter)—jumps far ahead in your career and addresses the questions of succession, particularly to your family's next generation. When should it happen, how can you help prepare a successor adult child(ren) for ongoing success, how do you exit gracefully?

File #9—Leaving the Office at the Office—is about ensuring you continue to invest in your own personal and mental well-being during the years you are driving intensely to make your business a success. Taking time for yourself, your family and your friends can add perspective to the business. Time away doesn't have to be a distraction or a magnet pulling you away.

File #2

Is Small Business Right for You?

Memo #3
To: Dan
Re: Epiphany, Spark, Passion

I NEVER CONSIDERED MYSELF A MOTIVATED STUDENT, sometimes far from it. In fact, when I was 17, I can vividly remember a conversation with my Dad and older brother in our garage where I relayed that I was thinking more about trade school than college. That's right, the garage, which in our home doubled as a workshop for all matter of projects led by "tinker-in-chief," Dad. I've always experienced when I am enjoying working with others on some project, it is a great time to share what else is on your mind. It seems to liberate the mind and people let their guard down, share more readily and perhaps are more thoughtful listeners and counselors.

My Dad also happened to be a high school teacher and our swim coach. I was being recruited to swim in college, like my older brother. He stressed the opportunity to be a part of a close-knit team, traveling and having your education partly funded. Like me, school did not come easily to Dad, but he sure worked hard over the years to give all his kids the opportunity to go to college.

Fast forward, I changed my major from Physical Education to Marketing—during my senior year, no less! Coaching was part of our family DNA, but as I neared the end of my swimming career, I felt it was time to look in a different direction. I made the leap to business because a licensed profession (i.e. medicine, law, engineering) was going to be much more of an effort than I was prepared to take on. Strategically, the marketing degree would require the least additional credit hours to gra duate. My observation was that effective marketing was often a key driver of a company's success. As a creative-type enjoying building things, I associated marketing to advertising to creativity. Validation arrived when my business class team won the semester's computer simulation game. Turned out, most of our efforts focused on the marketing and advertising of our business' product. There is nothing to sell if you don't let people know what you have. Luck maybe, but we did win. After six years, the kid who questioned going to college received a B.S. in Marketing!

In the spring of 1982, the U.S. economy was in the throes of the second helping of a double dip recession following President Reagan's wringing of inflation out of the economy. Nevertheless, K-Mart Corporation was recruiting for Management Trainees. K-Mart, retail, selling . . . Marketing! I interviewed and received an offer to join, eventually landing me in Gallup, New Mexico.

My K-Mart experience was probably too short to consider "learning on someone else's dime." It did, however, leave me with a general sense that I was playing an insignificant bit part coupled with just a feeling of being lost in the big corporate scene. For others, however, that is definitely not the case. They enjoy the ability to join colleagues in a training class and challenge each other as they learn the ways of the corporate world and thrive on the competition, both internal and external. In other professions, if you were an engineer by trade, maybe you need to start with a larger company that can provide the resources to foster your early design/build education. Sometimes, learning about a product, service, or skill in a larger company and being able to bring that experience to a new, or maybe even your own, company is a very viable and thoughtful career path.

Having made the decision to leave Gallup, New Mexico, I prepared to head back to my parent's home outside Chicago. Of course, this required a 2-day site-seeing tour of the American Southwest and Great Plains. Fortunately, I wasn't married, had no kids, and no college debt. Thus, the pressure to find immediate employment was slightly eased. My attitude at the time was that finding a "so-so" job out West was better than a decent job in a bummer location, but heading back to Denver with nothing on the line was also out of the question. Free rent at home with some time to think over my goals sounded like the best option. This time, however, instead of renting a U-Haul to take those worldly possessions home, I just stuffed my Honda Civic hatchback with what I could fit and left the rest behind—no more handmade water bed or whiskey barrel stereo cabinet. The K-Mart experience left some indelible marks on me, and the 1,481-mile trip home provided me plenty of time to reflect on what I liked and what I didn't. I thought I might try to use this period of solitude to begin formulating some ideas on what type of job to look for upon my arrival in Chicago.

It is quite possible my first indication of a desire to work in a small business came midway through my drive back home. In the middle of Oklahoma, my car suddenly began backfiring and sputtering. It was about 6 p.m. and I thought it best to pull over for the night and did so at the next exit just outside of Tulsa. I pulled into the first gas station I came to that looked like it would have a garage/mechanic. Given that it was the end of the day, I wasn't optimistic. The Civic limped into the station and then I saw I had happened upon one with no covered garage, there was only an outdoor lift. A young guy (younger than even my 23 years) walked out and asked how he could help. I gave him my expert summary of the symptoms complete with rather lame sound imitations. He had me pop the hood, pulled out one spark plug and says "you basically need a tune-up; you're driving this poor little car too hard."

He said he could do it right then instead of having me wait for the morning. I didn't need to be asked twice, so I let him have at it. The first thing he proceeded to do was call his wife and ask her to pick up four spark plugs and wires at the local auto parts store. Then, he turned to me and asked if I had eaten dinner. I replied no and he turned back to the phone and very politely asked his wife to bring sandwiches for us. Being from Chicago, the thought going through my mind was "this is not going to end well. My credit card is going to melt when he socks it to me and runs it through." At about 8 o'clock, sandwiches eaten, new plugs and wires installed, he turns to me and says "that'll be $25.00"—Wow, knock me over with a feather!!! I'm not a mechanic, but I figure parts alone were $25. Where's the labor, where's the dinner? I paid him double and I thought I was still getting a deal. As I drove away, that "poor little car" purred like a kitten. I remember thinking that was the best tune-up my Civic ever had.

Call it an epiphany, call it what you will. This experience left a hugely positive and lasting impression on me. I was so shocked. Here is this guy in a small one stall outdoor garage, his wife is his gofer and they just seemed so happy and nice. I remember thinking that this is the way all businesses should be. He was clearly doing what he loved, on his terms, in his way—and it seemed it was working out well. That must be a great feeling. Little did I know as I basked in my great fortune on day two of my drive, those thoughts would again be bouncing around in my head within the week.

When I arrived home, it just so happened my Dad knew of an open sales job at a small family-owned swimming products supplier he used. He wasn't exactly sure what this job would entail, but to him it was something he could suggest to help me get right back in the game.

So, I went to an interview only a couple of days after arriving home. While I was in talking to the owner, a woman walked in from the swimming pool design/build arm of the business (run by the owner's son) and tells him someone had just resigned and they need to quickly hire a replacement. The owner promptly said to her "well, talk to Todd here, he can do that for you." The rest, as they say, is history. I walked back with the woman to meet the owner's son in his office, he hired me, and I started up the following Monday! Mind you, this wasn't a case of taking the first thing that came along. My interest in trade school centered around designing and building things. I really felt this job could hold great promise because it addressed something in which I could feel a "passion." In addition, I'd have to listen to what clients wanted and then sell/market my ideas! Add to that, building swimming pools after spending the better part of 20 years swimming miles in them—well, talk about a fit!

My actual positon in the business was as an estimator, figuring the costs of building a pool already designed by the architects. We did design and build some of the deck equipment to our standards, but everything else within our projects was set to an architect's specs. At this entry level role, there was no customer sales aspect on my part, but I recognized I had to start somewhere.

This became what I would call my first real job. And, it was in a family business.

KEY TAKEAWAYS

- A "small business" is defined here as one run by a President who likely doubles as the Vice President of all the other functions

- Learning on "someone else's dime" is valuable pre-entrepreneurship training, but applicability will vary depending upon the size of the training ground and your career interests

- Impactful life experiences might well shed light on your core interests and passions

THERE ARE COUNTLESS ONLINE OR PROFESSIONAL TESTS you can take to dissect your personal styles and interests, your leadership traits, and any other manner of self-reflection. Over the years, when I interview prospective employees, I utilize a two-pronged assessment focused around a person's basic personal style and then their basic business management or working skills and style (see Memo #5).

As for your personal style and personal approach, there are a few key questions to ask yourself. I am certain the experts could raise several more and, depending on the type of business you are pursuing, you might identify some other traits uniquely appropriate to assess (per the graphic).

⟵ **Key Personality Traits Continuum** ⟶

- Risk Taking Tolerance
- Clarity of Vision - around what you want to do
- Salesmanship: Extrovert / Introvert
- Networking Effectiveness
- Competitiveness / Ambition
- Learning Goals and Learning Style
- Unwavering Determination
- Other Traits - unique to your business interests

Importantly, personality traits are not binary. That is, you don't either have them or not have them. Think of them all sitting along a continuum and your own possession of that trait may be stronger or less pronounced. For the sake of cutting to the heart of the matter, here is a set of traits upon which I focus.

Risk Taking Tolerance. What is your capacity and willingness to face challenges and uncertainty head on? Does the thought of this invigorate you or does it send a chill down your spine? In the words of President Bush #43's Defense Secretary Donald Rumsfeld:

> *"... as we know, there are known knowns; there are things we know we know. We also know there are known unknowns; that is to say we know there are some things we do not know. But there are also unknown unknowns—the ones we don't know we don't know."*

Before you become the driving force of the business, that is the owner /President, have you thoroughly analyzed and answered that question of "can I handle the pressure of making the key decisions?" You should further ask yourself if you are prepared to handle the ownership and CEO stress of providing the direction—and maybe even the financial capital—that the business requires.

As to the financial capital, startup or acquisition opportunities clearly have a cost of entry upfront. The personal question of how much financial capital you are prepared to invest and maintain at-risk is a critical question to resolve. For those entrepreneurs with families to support, this issue comes with a whole host of additional questions to ensure comfort and stability on the home front. In fact, it should very much become a two-person decision for entrepreneurs with spouses.

Clarity of Vision. Joining a small business will limit your exposure to the breadth and depth of business experiences available. The strategic business focus for a small company is inherently narrower than that for a larger corporation. Is this where you belong and will it most effectively challenge your skillset and interests? A $2 million revenue per year company is likely very focused; a $2 billion revenue per year company is likely to have multiple product or service lines, target markets, manufacturing processes and delivery channels, in-house administrative functions, etc. Thus, a career in small business may narrow your exposure to other potential areas of interest.

A small business career can, however, more readily serve as a springboard to a greater opportunity to explore the full range of roles and responsibilities required to manage a complete business enterprise. If the desire to learn what it takes to run "the whole show" or "be your own boss" is what you are after, the pathway of working in small business is going to provide the quickest route to that personal goal.

When my father-in-law, John, asked me to join Court Products, I felt I had the opportunity to learn from someone who had already become a successful businessman. I wasn't immediately thinking about becoming "my own boss," but I very much assessed the opportunity along the lines of things I liked: athletics, leisure, small, local, casual—all positive attributes to my line of interest.

At Court Products, I immediately felt I was a meaningful part of the big picture. I felt more engaged because it enabled me to be more attuned to everything going on within the company. For the most part, in a small business, the entire company is sitting right there within "those four walls." A single K-Mart store was multiples larger than the physical premises of any of my subsequent small business jobs. Within a small business office, you tend to see everything and hear everything. Most decisions have some level of impact on everyone in the company, not just a division or department.

This aspect of being able to impact the whole business can be a positive motivation. It can drive the energy level behind your performance. You actually feel you matter. You will be handed tasks to complete and only you—no team, no assistant—are expected to complete them. The first time this realization hits you, it can make you feel like you are out on an island alone. When done right, however, it is a great feeling of accomplishment in that you readily see your effort and results made a difference for the entire company.

Another aspect of small business ownership and leadership some entrepreneurs forget is that they start a business focused around perhaps that one great idea, product or service and think they will continue to work just on that and that alone. Reality soon enters into this notion as the need to design, build, market, administer, service, etc. suddenly becomes apparent. That all must be attended to. Not necessarily by you, but certainly under your direction and leadership. That may take your eye off the ball in terms of what drove you to create your own business initially.

Salesmanship: Extrovert/Introvert. As noted, I believe that if you cannot effectively communicate what you have to sell, you will sell nothing. Said another way, you must be the chief advocate of your product or service in order to create the belief there is value in what you represent.

Salesmanship, however, isn't just about the business' core products or services. Anyone must be prepared to sell any number and manner of ideas, decisions, choices, etc. throughout their personal and business lives. In fact, I firmly believe the #1 product anyone must perfect selling is themselves. If you cannot master that effort, attaining the best out of opportunities, relationships and anything else becomes greatly complicated.

You have very likely at some point taken a "test" to determine your social or interactive style akin to a Myers-Briggs indicator. Simplifying this type of assessment, on one end of the continuum are the extroverts. They are the outgoing, outspoken folks that enjoy being around and talking to others and think on their feet as they communicate. They tend to draw their energy by having a focus on engaging with others. While they may count many as friends, the depth of those relationships may not be so intense.

Contrast that to the other end of the continuum, the introverts. They are not hermits, but may prefer some valuable alone time to reflect on their current thoughts and issues. They tend to think things over before speaking out. Introverts tend to enjoy a tighter circle of friends and business colleagues with whom they might develop stronger, deeper relationships.

Effectively selling your company's vision and your daily decisions to your teammates will probably become one of your most frequent sales efforts. Know your style and know your teammates' personalities in order to maximize your success. Selling your business story to your external business partners like vendors, bankers, investors is equally important. It requires a thoughtful degree of preparation with a commitment to a professional and balanced approach and style.

Effective selling means also being able to handle rejection. Can you re-package your ideas, product or service and complete a partial sale? Nothing is gained by expressing an abrupt and overt negative reaction which could ruin any hope of a future sale. Know how you handle rejection in other situations and think about how you may need to change your behavior to be effective for your business.

Networking Effectiveness. Networking is a conscious effort at professionally reaching out to expand one's own horizons with the intent to provide the same to others in a mutually productive relationship. Networking may not always provide the opportunity to "scratch each other's back," but good networkers recognize the notion of paying it forward. Per the previous topic, being an extrovert does not guarantee success at networking. In fact, extroverts may find they should dial back a forceful public persona to develop more meaningful relationships. Further, while it may be more of a personal challenge for a natural introvert to get out of their comfort zone and establish connections, a tightly focused productive network can be very reassuring and rewarding.

As a small business, you will naturally have fewer customers, vendors and external providers of professional services than a typical large corporation. That does not mean this potentially narrower list of business contacts couldn't become a very valuable and enriching source of market information. Make a point to understand how some of your major customers and vendors network across your industry. There may be helpful small business conferences or trade shows to attend where you can broaden your reach. Join your community's Rotary Club, merchants' association or business roundtable. As you do so, this will improve your flow of information and knowledge into your business and hopefully lead to greater success.

Competitiveness/Ambition. As the owner of a small business, you must demonstrate the motivation to drive the business every day; exerting energy and leadership as an example for the team. If that is not your nature, you are quite likely in the wrong career. Problems may be awaiting you just around the corner. Your motivation should be grounded in a healthy competitive outlook—one that strives for success in all facets of the business at all times.

Some businesses thrive on creating a competitive culture to spur incremental accomplishments. Think of the often cited "sales goals" mantra in many companies. As long as this can be kept healthy and doesn't degenerate into destructive behavior on the part of various individuals or teams, competition within a business can be positive and lead to great success.

Within a small business, where only a handful of individuals would be pitted against one another, creating an environment where one person or faction routinely outshines another is a prescription for disruptive office relationships. The smaller the team, the greater the need to create the competitive focus on external matters and team goals where your company's employees can take collective pride in winning.

I mentioned I was a swimmer. Aside from a couple of relays and the absolute need to have teammates to train with in order to maintain sanity, swimming is an individual sport. You really are testing yourself on a daily basis and the ever-present clock measures your progress. While I worked against that clock in practice, I knew I would have those head-to-head races and I had to be as prepared as possible. I see it just the same in business—you must continue to work hard to be the best you can be, otherwise someone else will surely be nipping at your heels.

Competition can drive political behavior, and office politics can occur anywhere. It is certainly not limited by the size of an office, per se. Probability of factions increase as the size of an organization grows. Getting on the right side of the boss can become a national pastime in large organizations where the ability to surreptitiously maneuver via various avenues borders on designation as a full contact sport. In a small business, such behavior should be fairly observable and needs to be squelched by the boss to promote team unity. Turning a blind eye toward political maneuvers within your small business is likely to create a toxic environment and complicate your company's path to success.

Learning Goals and Learning Style. In small business, the responsibility to maintain or learn new valuable and translatable business and management skills largely falls upon you. There are no training departments, there are no corporate-wide mentor programs and there is no guaranty that within the small number of teammates one can find a good coach/mentor.

Following my transition from K-Mart to the pool business, my most important learning discovery was appreciating the sum total it takes to run a complete business. Even the little things that wouldn't normally pop into one's mind were eye openers. In a small business office, it is all right there in front of you to observe every day. Processing all that at the pool business was my learning opportunity. That came on top of my assigned responsibilities as a project estimator. I may not have seen everything done the "right" way, but I was seeing all that needed to get done and the order of importance assigned to various tasks and decisions.

Because you see everything, you can't help but witness both positives and negatives. The key is, learn from both. Over the years, I've often heard "learn these 'positives' so you will remember them and take them with you wherever you may go next." Learning, however, isn't just about trying to do something correct in repetition. It is also knowing enough to avoid doing something yet again in a way you previously discovered did not produce the desired result. I have several times found myself doing something one way because I remember it did NOT work the other way when I saw it or experienced it elsewhere. Therefore, I do make a point of learning from the "negatives" and keep those with me to ensure I don't attempt a repeat. It is a tough thing for younger people to learn given the heavy teaching focus on simply replicating positives. Within Court Products, we are not afraid to soak up both positives and negatives to lead us toward both what to do as well as what not to do.

When it comes to learning, some people are more visual or tactile learners, eyes-on or hands-on, as opposed to auditory learners gaining knowledge through discussion or lecture. As someone interested in designing and building things, I always liked to lay things out visually and get involved in the process. Your learning style may also influence your ability to contribute and communicate. Within your small business, however, giving thought to the type of learner and teacher you are—and similarly the people you hire—may facilitate how well you can communicate your vision and execute your operational strategy. Not being aware can lead to the proverbial "ships passing in the night" on critical office communication and training.

Unwavering Determination. You have heard the saying "Rome wasn't built in a day." Same goes for building your own company into a well-tuned machine capable of achieving your goals and earning you a comfortable living. Building a company around the product or service idea you have developed is going to introduce you to a wide range of tasks that require various levels of mastery. You won't master each of them the first time out, and you definitely should not throw in the towel on the first sign of difficulty. It is virtually guaranteed to be a roller-coaster ride in the early days. If you are going to make the effort to start or buy your own company, you had better have a "can do" attitude. There should be no time for regrets later in life saying "if only I had just stayed with it a little longer . . .." To avoid those regrets, the early days are going to require a great deal of hard work mixed with healthy doses of patience.

Just for a moment, think of all the activities you have completed so far today and how many of those required a level of patience to allow for completion. Waiting for your morning coffee, waiting for the hot water to come on in the shower, waiting on a few red lights, etc. You get the point. Now start a new business and think of all the brand-new tasks that must be accomplished each day and how you want them done perfectly—and quickly. Patience, persistence and determination are a must for the small business owner.

It is valuable to really ask yourself what motivates you, what excites you, what gets you out of bed every morning to tackle each new day.

It is human nature to become bored with routines. To maintain our interest, we look for ways to get better, develop new skills and continue our personal growth. These motivations may very well change over time driven by age, family status, etc. How you get there and with whom will likely evolve over time. What cannot change, however, is the sustained high level of commitment it takes to lead a successful small business enterprise.

KEY TAKEAWAYS

- As owner, you will also own *all* the risk; is the unknown invigorating or agonizing?

- The singular idea behind your business needs to be supported by your commitment to running the business operations that support it

- Nobody is either an extrovert or introvert; know your tendencies to enhance your effectiveness

- By definition, a small business owner has a more limited sphere of contacts; cultivate them

- Join organizations that bring small business owners together to exchange ideas and best practices

- Focus your competitive instincts and those of your team externally, not on each other

- Know how you learn, it is probably how you teach— and you are the head of training

- Learn to identify how your teammates learn; it is probably different from you and may require an alternative training method

- Appreciate patience and persistence will be necessary as you launch your new endeavor

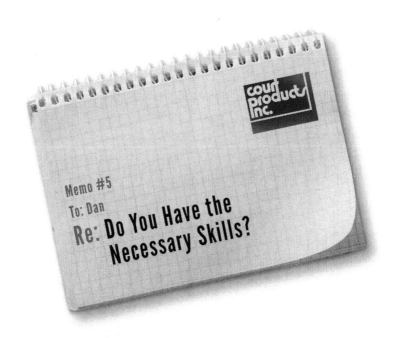

Memo #5
To: Dan
Re: Do You Have the Necessary Skills?

YOU ARE OFF TO A GOOD START if your personality traits (Memo #4) provide a good fit within the small business working world. Just the same, those who enter this arena must either possess or develop certain skills to effectively run their own business. For that, I think the following basic managerial skills are necessary to be successful. Mind you, nobody is proficient at everything, but the successful small business owner/operator must know his or her own strengths and weaknesses.

Your company will be based around your business idea which you should know in great detail. For example, don't expect to open an architectural practice designing new homes if you lack an engineering or design background. It is very common to focus on developing other administrative business skills over time while at first contracting out for certain professional assistance, such as accounting services, legal help, etc. Do not let your lack of familiarity with all business administrative skills hold you back from launching your company and seizing a great opportunity.

Just as the Memo #4 exercise around your inherent personality traits was not intended to be exhaustive, the skillsets set forth below are just to challenge you as you begin to rate your business and management attributes. Consider whether there are any additional unique attributes you should add to the list that would help drive success in your chosen industry. Similar to the personality traits, do not look at any of these skills as binary. That is, whether you have "perfected" them or not. Rather, again think of the range as a continuum. You will have some of these skills and attributes that lean one way or another, it doesn't mean you are one OR the other. It is important, however, to understand your weaknesses or development needs so that you seek appropriate assistance and expertise when required.

Key Business / Management Skills Continuum

- Leader / Follower
- Core Competencies
- Listener / Talker
- Do-er / Delegator
- Team Player / Lone Wolf
- Other Skills - unique to your business interests

Leader/Follower. In a small business where more often than not "the leader" is the owner, that person must be prepared to create an environment where the team believes in his or her confidence, direction and decisiveness. Importantly, leadership should not solely be thought of as decision making in this case. In a small business, the Leader/Owner is the embodiment of the core values that will either drive the company to success or have it wander in mediocrity. Think of it as not only "talking the talk," but also very much "walking the walk."

Many large organizations are tabbed with having a slow, lumbering, bureaucratic decision making process. One benefit of a small business is that there are fewer people and management layers through which decisions must travel. When challenges or problems arise, the benefit of a small business is the leaders can quickly get to a resolution. Here is the caveat, however, the "big decision(s)"-maker in the small business is typically the owner. If the team doesn't have confidence in that person, or share a common view of the business, they don't have an appeals route. If that owner also tends toward being indecisive, the decision-making stops completely and can be very hard on the business—both from a financial and a team morale perspective. Worse yet, employees may question their commitment to staying as they lose the empowerment of being part of a decision-making process.

Be mindful, as well, all decisions have consequences. Some decisions have known consequences, others may have detrimental unintended consequences. In your mind, your decision analysis should focus first on the impact to your customer, then on you and your team.

Another critical aspect of leadership and decision making in a small business is that there is nobody else to blame when your invested financial capital begins to wither away. It's your call, you have to make it, period.

Finally, while leaders lead teams, the leader in a small business also has to be a solid team player. In the first small company I worked in, the president of the business was struggling with some personal issues. The impact on the business was immediate given the decision-making structure in place. That is, projects would stagnate and nothing moved forward without his say. We were in the middle of jobs and hit some crisis that required his involvement and we wouldn't get an answer for days. It took a devastating toll on both our reputation and our team morale. The project manager would rightfully become frustrated with the delays in decision-making and would venture off on his own and make decisions which translated into further arguments and gridlock at the top. There must be definite leadership, direction and decision-making at the top or at least a clear mandate as to the delegation of decision-making through the ranks. Your team may not always agree with what comes down from the top, but at least they will have confidence in where you are headed and how you intend on getting there.

Core Competencies. If you google small businesses offered for sale, you will see an overwhelming array of companies and the stuff they make and stuff they do for people or other businesses. Interestingly, however, if you look at most of these opportunities, they are focused around a singular product, technical competency or service approach. The question you have to ask yourself is where does your skillset fit in? It may be a moot point because you have already designed the wonder widget that solves a particular problem of the masses or you have a particular skill at knowing all about flooring options and quality installation. In other cases, such as mine, Court Products sells other brand name manufacturers' products, just as other wholesalers might. We must then differentiate ourselves by knowing who our customers are, what they want, creating it and delivering it when they need it. We have built our company around the notion that GREAT CUSTOMER SERVICE MATTERS.

Some may question whether providing "great customer service" should be viewed as a core competency. In a more concrete sense, our marketing approach supplemented by our relentless competitive drive are the critical core competencies serving the customer. Breaking it down, I greatly admire the respective missions of the clubs and organizations that comprise our customer base. I compare and study the products we sell, how they are used, how they have evolved. I also have a strong desire to continuously improve and build upon my own skills. Looking at each of these aspects of our business, I knew there could be plenty of other people out there with the same level of respect, the same level of interest, the same access to the manufacturers, and so on. I had to differentiate and knew my competitiveness would enable us to distinguish ourselves by providing the glue that holds it all together—great customer service.

For those schooled in a technical competency such as architectural engineering or pharmacy, building a business around such training starts with your professional credentials. Without credentials, you would have to hire the experts and become manager of the business—if that concept would even fly with those professionals. Some areas of proficiency you can develop over time. Perhaps you have gained expertise in computer hardware and software and could create an information technology consulting service for home users. Then again, maybe you have developed strong management skills and can find an opportunity where organizing and motivating a team is primary to the subject matter expertise of the underlying product or service, such as a franchisee.

Listener/Talker. In a small business, when something goes "off plan," as it often does, it can quickly magnify the overall impact on the business and the team. If I were to make a habit of ignoring or talking over the general observations, inputs and ideas of the team, I have virtually shut off the flow of information and creativity throughout the entire business. Don't be that problem.

As a small business owner, you can't afford to shut down the voices of your teammates or you are destined for failure. Your pipeline of observations about what works, or what requires adjustment, becomes bottlenecked around your own ego. Listening out for those things that are working well is equally important as those that require adjustment because you also need to know when to seize the advantage in the market.

Similarly, your tendency toward being a listener or a talker can influence your decision-making style and effectiveness. In Stephen Covey's best-selling *The 7 Habits of Highly Effective People*, he reminds us to:

Seek first to understand, then to be understood.

For external feedback, we encourage our team to solicit customer feedback on all facets of our business during routine interactions. A thoughtfully designed, non-intrusive customer satisfaction survey can also be used on occasion. Company performance can be enhanced if you are all good listeners and can pull in valuable customer feedback.

Do-er/Delegator. This is that question about whether you are willing to get your fingernails dirty. Let's face it, we all know some people that prefer to "manage." Preferring to do so doesn't mean that one is actually great at doing so. In fact, most good managers are those that spent their time in the trenches learning core skills and knowledge so that they understand the implications of their directives. And if those good managers happen to have been an external hire, their ability to translate effective leadership in a new company is also likely due to strong listening skills in their transplanted environment.

At Court Products, every so often I spend a day in every one of my employee's positions. This helps me maintain an understanding of what we are doing across the business functions and how we are getting it done. It is particularly helpful when we need to adapt to changes in the business environment and decisions must be made about the "what" and "how." It is not so much gaining empathy for my team as it is to help me make more effective operational changes and decisions. Sometimes those changes are at their suggestion. And, to be sure, there is no guarantee that just because you are the boss and you spent a day in their chair, that everyone will fall in line with every decision you make.

We once re-ordered the flow of our warehouse designed to facilitate the natural flow of picking an order, packing it and preparing it for shipment. I included the team in the process and they favorably accepted the change. On the other hand, one year I alone made the call to update our computer software at year-end. That happens to be our busiest time of the year and the update was disruptive. In retrospect, that decision was from an autocratic delegator that should have gained more appreciation of the potential drawbacks from those better versed in the demands of the daily routines during peak season.

Team Player/Lone Wolf. During the Great Recession (late 2007-2009), as Court Products struggled every day to maintain our importance to our customers, we had to face the reality that demand had softened. In many businesses, as the top line weakens, an immediate and higher emphasis is placed on controlling costs. One of our employees raised the idea that we could save $150 month if instead of contracting out our cleaning services, we did it ourselves—that's right, including our toilets. Well, we adopted that teamwork suggestion, including my own spot in the rotation. That was an extreme example, but you would never expect anyone in a 50-person or larger company to believe they would ever end up with janitorial services in their job description.

The reality of the lower headcount in a small business environment is another factor in the critical nature of teamwork. At Court Products, we currently have six employees. If one person is out ill or on vacation, our workforce is reduced by 16.7%! Not many businesses function well when that shortfall occurs. Thus, preparing the team to learn and assume a wider array of tasks and responsibilities is essential.

Pull back the focus just a bit. Teamwork gets loads of attention at any company, big or small. The issue as I see it, however, is that in larger companies, if the team is not working well together, the members can be altered. When you have six people in the office, the ability to readily interchange players is severely restricted. Thus, the premium on strong team players is critical. It is truly a "one for all" mentality in a small business office, there is just no compromise. As such, you need to set the tone as a team player and be able to work through difficult situations by demonstrating balance and flexibility. I'm not advocating capitulating on every instance, rather your ability to sell your ideas to your teammates is something you must grow and develop from Day 1.

KEY TAKEAWAYS

- Small businesses require clear leadership and direction from the top with delegation as appropriate

- Focus your company around what you bring to the table; your primary area of expertise/knowledge

- The information pipeline for a small business owner comes from the customer and the team—listen carefully when they speak out

- As the owner, you will have to hire others to help execute, know and appreciate what you ask of them

- By definition, small business teams must develop an "all for one" culture

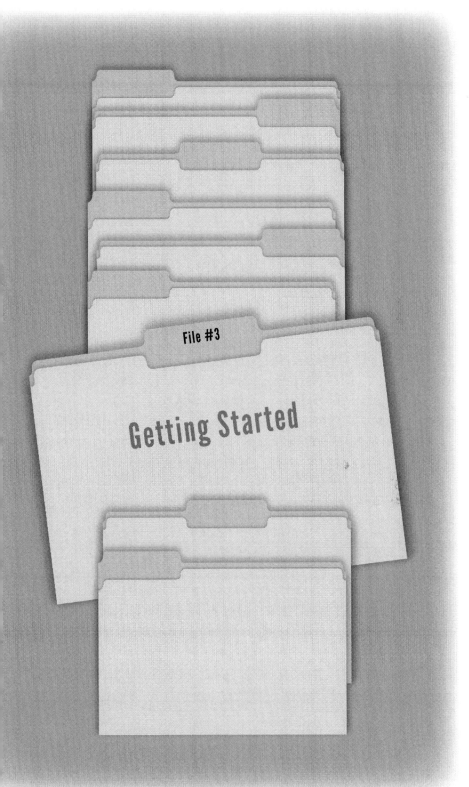

File #3

Getting Started

Memo #6
To: Dan
Re: Build, Buy or Transform

EVERY PRESIDENTIAL ELECTION SEASON, candidates of both parties make a point to pander to the small business community. In fact, some mention the majority of jobs in America are jobs in the small business sector. This may not be true, pending your definition of small. Census Bureau data through 2015 suggests that companies with 100 or fewer employees employ just over one-third (34.3%) of all U.S. workers. This percentage has trended down from over 40% in the mid-1980s.

In terms of business formations, during the 1980's, roughly 12.5% of all firms were less than one year old. New business formations are an indication of small business activity as they are typically smaller start-up enterprises. Following the Great Recession, that level is now running about 7.5% to 8.5%. In 2015, the Labor Department reported there were approximately 680,000 new businesses started with an average employment of only 4 ½ persons! In fact, since the early 1990s, the typical small business startup has declined from an average of 7 employees to the present 4 ½.

While the recent trends may not be as favorable to small businesses and small business employment, the fact remains there are vast numbers of people employed in the sector and living out their dreams of running their own show.

It would be great to claim that the entire spectrum of businesses out there is open for you to choose your specific interest, but that is clearly not the case. If you don't have your own idea upon which to launch a business, buying an existing company matching your critical interests is complicated by these facts: 1) finding companies in your field of interest; 2) a company for sale that can benefit from your skillsets; and 3) both of these hitting at the same time.

In my early career, my confidence level and risk tolerance for buying my own business just wasn't strong enough. In addition, in the 1980's, the available information on potential business-for-sale opportunities was just not as accessible as today's online offerings. Having had some success at running my own company, it has been interesting to note over the last decade or so how many business brokers now come to me with opportunities. You can virtually sign up with a business broker as easily as a real estate broker. Attorneys and accountants are additional sources of potential buying opportunities.

Of course, if you have generated that particular idea that can support building your own business, you won't have to worry about the availability of acquisition opportunities. As an entrepreneur, however, you cannot bank on every idea being the one to win or last forever. Whether you start or buy your own business, you have to be ready to re-invent yourself and stay ahead of changing market conditions. Even franchisees experience longer term cyclicality in their core product—think of the healthy alternatives impact to the fast food sector.

Building a new company around your idea requires thoughtful planning. Understand, however, whether your product or your idea requires a rapid introduction into the market. If so, consider partnering with an existing company to help quickly launch your concept into the market. If you have time to plan, consider a wealth of sources to help guide you through the detailed technical start-up steps. The U.S. Government's Small Business Administration (SBA) maintains a website at http://www.sba.gov/ with a wealth of guidance on many of these detailed start-up requirements questions.

In my case, however, it really ended up becoming the old adage that sometimes the opportunity chooses you. By choice or by happenstance, taking on such a role requires strong due diligence so as to avoid what could be a disastrous near term retreat. In subsequent Memos #8 to #10, approaches to due diligence will be covered in greater detail.

My own career at the swimming pool design firm was largely relegated to a back-office role calculating project specifics and costs. I had hoped to actually be in on the sales side and working with clients to design something to their needs and wishes. In fact, I eventually left the first small firm and joined a quasi-competitor in a sales role. I was teamed with a perfectly nice gentleman who took life at a decidedly slower pace than me. He would drive both of us to our customer visits and, despite his desire to severely under challenge any posted speed limit, he always owned the left lane whenever two were available. People would come up behind us and honk and he would make this curious looping hand gesture inside the car and utter "go over me!" Of course, they would eventually pass on the right and I would end up the object of their scorn.

Months passed and I can't say I ever came home raving about how great work had been and how it was speeding me within reach of my professional goals. Then, the big break came when I was handed a lead on a new pool. It was a restaurant owner—so a personal job. That was fine by me as long as I had the opportunity to run point. As it turned out, that point was a sharp jab as this guy wanted to build a koi pond in the front of his restaurant!

As I increasingly evaluated—and questioned—my situation at this second swimming pool design/build firm, my father-in law's (John) business was now losing money as recreational preferences had moved away from racquetball. He had invested in racquetball clubs during the era of the racquetball craze (late 1970s to mid 1980s). The clubs also sold a modest array of equipment, apparel, shoes, etc. His number two guy, I'll call him Bill, had also just given notice that he would be leaving for a role at a larger public sporting goods manufacturer. John and Bill had worked together for ten years and Bill was actually able to provide John nearly six months' notice.

John, from whom I learned that it was highly valuable to create a network of dependable people you could use as a sounding board on matters of all types, had worked with some of his close confidantes to evaluate his next steps. John basically decided he could 1) shut the doors; 2) hire someone he didn't know as a turnaround expert; or 3) ask Todd (yeah, me) to help stabilize the company. To his credit, John was concerned about how bringing a son-in-law into a stressed business situation could impact our relationship. He initially held a few thoughtful private conversations with my wife. Isn't it just like a couple of men not being able to sit down and flesh it out directly, huh!

In the "do as I say, not as I do" advice category, here is another excuse for my notable lack of due diligence. Consider whether you would be prepared to ask your father-in-law to see his financials for the last few years and spend a few weeks asking all manner of detailed and prying questions. Playing it out, let's just say you did have the guts to do that. And, then, of all things, let's say you decided "sorry, the business is not good enough for me!" I felt like I had placed myself squarely between the proverbial rock and a hard place.

In my defense, I did think through a few key points of personal interest as to "fit." The business served an athletic related market, remaining in line with my strong interests in recreation and athletics. My general view from prior family discussion was that Court Products was primarily a distribution company. I am one of those visual learners and thinkers, not the auditory type that uses more of the listening/reading learning processes. As we spoke, I had already begun mapping out flows of product and activity within the company. Evidence demonstrated this wasn't one of their strengths. There was a sizeable room filled with unmarked boxes and nothing even remotely resembling a tracking system in order to locate product to fill a customer order.

Many ideas began popping into my head. I was aware distributors in many industries are often swallowed up by either end of the food chain—that is, their vendors or their customers. In order to survive, marketing our core competency and defending it with energy and passion would be the keys to keeping our head above water. I believed these necessities would play to my traits and skills.

KEY TAKEAWAYS

- If it is your idea, prepare to build a company or partner up

- If you just seek to run a company, there is a large universe of existing opportunities

- Any opportunity requires extensive due diligence in order to screen appropriately; don't let enthusiasm overshadow a thoughtful decision-making process

- Even after a few years of operating, to stay ahead, you must monitor the environment and prepare to alter your original course

IN FILE #2 (IS SMALL BUSINESS RIGHT FOR YOU?), we talked about a basic and somewhat broad-based view of your personality traits (Memo #4) and your business and management skills (Memo #5). It is very much worth the effort to evaluate your small business opportunities against this inventory of traits and skills.

But where does one begin when you consider the shear multitude of options out there? These could range from the proprietary ideas dreamed up every day in people's minds to the businesses currently listed for sale through brokers, bankers or online. You cannot be expected to know everything about every possible business opportunity that may interest you. To borrow some wisdom from the imminently successful billionaire investor, Warren Buffet:

> *"Never invest in a business you cannot understand."*

And further:

> *"Risk comes from not knowing what you're doing."*

So, while your traits and skills require careful evaluation, so does your inherent knowledge base.

For someone that is very financially conservative, a turnaround may not be the most appropriate starting point should you wish to maintain blood pressure at less than stratospheric levels. Maybe retail foodservice as a franchisee is a goal and you learn better in a structured environment. The financially conservative individual might fit better in an established company where corporate support via standard equipment and knowledge sharing is legendary—say, McDonalds and the ability to learn at Hamburger U.

		XYZ Manufacturing	ABC Retail Service
Personality Traits	**Risk Taking Tolerance**	High equipment costs; market likes product	Low entry cost; must constantly find new customers
	Clarity of Vision	Love to see physical product of my efforts	Repeat business reflects strong work
	Salesmanship: Extrovert / Introvert	Selling is product based	Lack sales skill person to person
	Networking Effectiveness	Industry connections	Retail is advertising driven
	Competitiveness / Ambition	Very high	Less critical; only one in town
	Learning Style	Very visual process/product	Need to listen to customers
	Unwavering Determination	This is my invention	Best alternative or true passion?
Business Skills	**Leader / Follower**	Quality oriented team	Can rely on sales manager
	Core Competencies	Organized; skilled machinist	Business school background
	Listener / Talker	This is my idea; must try to be open	Listen to learn; but not a salesperson
	Do-er / Delegator	Ready to dig in; but also need to lead / strategize	Ability to lead when not in a customer facing role?
	Team Player / Lone Wolf	Recognize need to cover key skills	Will be coach of sales team

Set forth down one side of a blank page the various personality traits and skillsets discussed in Memos #4 and #5, along with others you feel uniquely describe you as a person. List a few businesses or business types across the top to create a grid. Then patiently and honestly work through the grid inserting short comments to describe the fit. You may wish to include a spouse, close friend or colleague that can also provide another perspective to ensure you are seeing the opportunity from all angles.

KEY TAKEAWAYS

- Understand before you invest; otherwise, your financial health may suffer greatly

- Create a grid of your traits and skills vs. those it takes to succeed in various types of businesses

Memo #8
To: Dan
Re: Strategic Analysis

AS MENTIONED, I JOINED COURT PRODUCTS without an exhaustive due diligence effort and evolved with the company over three challenging, and sometimes painful, years. Had I carefully thought through John's initial invitation to join the company, I quite possibly would have said "no, thanks all the same, John."

With my plan for the new Court Products, I now had a chance to use the last three years of learning in the job to more thoughtfully evaluate future prospects. While I wasn't quite so formal, below are some analytical due diligence approaches worthy of any entrepreneur's initial investment of time—and capital. Due diligence is an important term for a small business owner. It's a reasonable standard of care one invests in a comprehensive review of an investment opportunity. Think of it as the "look before you leap" requirement.

When the subject of investing in a startup or buying an existing business arises, people tend to jump too quickly to the numbers. What is the cash flow, what are the sales, what are the margins, what are the assets? Valid questions, to be sure; however, how do you determine this? How do you create a viable financial projection with assumptions rooted in realistic and plausible scenarios?

Sometimes, the best advice you receive was something you learned long ago—from Mom. I can remember her asking sometimes "who, what, where, when, why and how" as some issue arose requiring resolution of one sort or another. To that inventor of the wonder widget or the provider of that highly-valued service, you should attempt to answer those questions my Mom posed. You then would have a pretty comprehensive view of the viability of the value of your idea as the core of a business enterprise. Who is your target market? What problem or need does it solve, what benefit does it provide, what does it compete with or replace? Where can you produce it, store it, sell it? When do customers need it, can you deliver it? Why do you want to do this? How will you provide this?

In the final analysis, you need to be comfortable in the view that your customers can learn the benefits of your company's product or service and how it is better than other alternatives. Your customers must value your product or service in a manner that drives sufficient demand to sustain a profitable business. Granted, sometimes you may need to force feed your customers with education in the form of expert marketing. Not every product or service on offer comes with a ready demand awaiting fulfillment.

Analytical Frameworks. There are also more polished and professionally thought out frameworks for this important analysis. Illustrated below is one such tightly and thoughtfully-designed framework originally published by Michael Porter in 1979 in the Harvard Business Review. This is an intuitive and straightforward framework describing virtually any business analysis—acquisition, investment, expansion. Further, whether it is the analysis behind a start-up, a financial investment or the ongoing strategic planning one must execute, the framework is well-suited to helping guide a small business through the necessary elements of a diligent and comprehensive analysis and review. As you think through the various elements of the framework, it is important to consider the broad array of factors affecting each party's environment, i.e. regulatory, technological, environmental, etc.

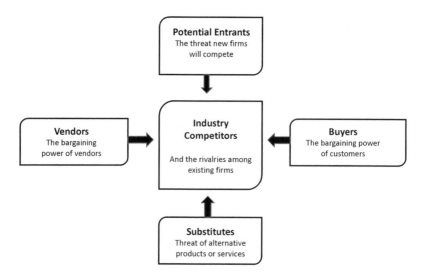

You can search the internet for a wide range of acronym-laced analytical frameworks to use:

SWOT—Strengths, Weaknesses, Opportunities, Threats.

PESTLE—Political, Economic, Sociological, Technological, Legal, Environmental

If your business has unique attributes that require more in-depth analysis, i.e. environmental issues, then maybe an alternative approach like PESTLE is better suited.

For Day 1 and Ongoing. Either way, the intent is to deconstruct your business approach and your business environment, generate awareness of market ebbs and flows and strategic moves of key constituencies in order to better position your company to respond proactively (and profitably) to inevitable change. Think about how valuable that analysis is prior to buying or launching a new small business. Not only do you undertake a dry run at some of the potential early pitfalls and potholes, you are doing double duty by formulating a written strategy to guide the early days of your business and your team.

The ability to improve your analysis of your business and the competitive landscape will undoubtedly improve over time—provided you keep your eyes and ears open. Your vendors are a great source of information, not just by what they might tell you, but also how they act. We often have vendors alert us to new developments we can pass along in our product offering. We also have had a few vendors (who are no longer partners) that we discovered had begun to end-run us to segments of our customer base. As mentioned, where margins are tight, the supply chain will attempt to squeeze out those elements not perceived to be adding value. Court Products is adding value.

Similarly, your customers are not likely to explicitly tell you exactly what you want to know about their other vendors, thus part of this strategic analysis is carefully dissecting your own sales data. How have buying patterns or volumes changed? Do regional differences exist that must be accounted for in product or service offering? Your own business will collect a wealth of data that requires periodic review to ensure it remains healthy.

KEY TAKEAWAYS

- Arriving at a confident financial investment value first requires an understanding of the business and its market environment

- Deconstruct how a business operates to understand the key linkages and dependencies

- Use the analysis as a dry run to identify future challenges; it is preparation for a written strategy

- Once operational, the data you collect should feed ongoing refinements of your analysis

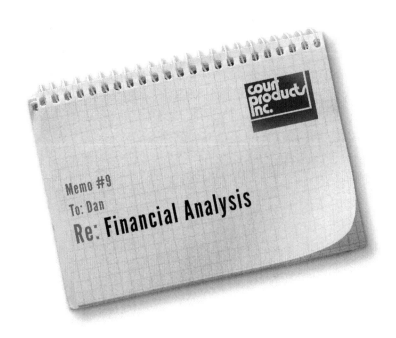

Memo #9
To: Dan
Re: Financial Analysis

AS THE OLD SAYING GOES, the cart should not be placed before the horse. Once you have thoroughly vetted the strategic aspects of your business and the factors that influence your ability to produce and sell your product or service, you will now be on more stable footing to create a set of viable financial plans and understand the financial opportunity ahead. You will have better foresight into sales potential, costs to drive that volume of business, investment required to deliver the product or service, etc. It should all flow with a higher level of understanding, confidence and justification.

Your business could very well be a 10, 20, 30+ year career investment, maybe even an eventual family fortune. And while the degree of certainty with respect to projecting a long term financial business plan declines as you work your way out your projection horizon, you must make that effort to thoughtfully plan out the early years to avoid a potential catastrophic beginning.

Valuation Methods. Starting from the top on the revenue line, one of the more difficult aspects of evaluating an existing business for purchase is the ability to retain the customer base. Consider, for example, buying a major franchise operation. In this case, the "halo" of the national (or perhaps global) corporation continues to provide the image to the customer. It is, however, up to your specific franchise to deliver on the scripted experience. Alternatively, consider a young dentist buying out a practice. How does (s)he or how can (s)he ensure that the customer base will be retained? Was there a special connection to the retiring doctor such that many patients will feel far less committed to return?

When buying a business where the ability to retain the customer base is questionable, it may be best to structure some form of earn out in your purchase arrangement. An earn out provides a seller an agreed amount of additional compensation if the business achieves agreed upon sales or financial targets. This approach maintains the seller's engagement thereby improving the potential of providing for a smooth transition. In addition, if the buyer retains the customer base, likely the value of the business is retained and then everybody wins. Conversely, if revenue suffers from business moving elsewhere, the buyer is not overpaying for a business model that wasn't readily transferable.

As you contemplate the financial model you might build for a small business, recognize it is not a public company with stores of readily available information on revenues, growth rates, costs/margins, investment requirements, etc. Further, sellers of businesses will be reluctant to readily make available the answers to the questions you might have for fear of not reaching a deal and feeling as though they have given away the combination to the company safe. Nevertheless, careful thought given to this analysis can prepare you well if negotiating to buy a business. Sources such as business brokers or community bankers may be able to provide effective guidance. Don't overlook the ability to gain your own insights for your business model from the data available online at websites like http://www.bizbuysell.com/.

There are two other approaches worth mentioning given the dearth of detailed financial information that may exist in the market for small businesses. One is a comparable company approach. Perhaps there are very clear comparables; again, think of franchisees where a large corporation has data on values of business that have sale prices relative to various benchmarks like revenue or cash flow. Similarly, you could review parallel companies currently in the market to test your assumptions of value. A review of bizbuysell.com provides prices offered including figures for revenue, cash flow, assets, facilities and employee counts. If you can't find an exact match, evaluate comparable types of distributors, retailers or service organizations that mirror your company but recognize that depending upon the exact product or service, the revenue opportunity and margins may vary which could lead to meaningful differences in value.

A third approach, which could arise for both investing or start-up situations, is an asset purchase. In cases where an existing business failed (hopefully understanding why), buying the physical assets to launch your own company may be a very opportune purchase. In manufacturing settings, perhaps the plant and equipment exist and you seek to bring your own proprietary dies to produce your invention. In the case of Court Products, when I took over the business to focus exclusively on the national not-for-profit clubs and service organizations, John and I agreed on a purchase price primarily for the inventory related to that segment. We also valued the "bones" of the company at a modest value since all the administrative infrastructure was in place and operational—a very helpful advantage to be up and running particularly when initiating a turnaround plan.

Understanding the accounting of your business, the drivers of sales and costs, is critical to performing a sound financial analysis. It can be overwhelming to sift through and find all those key drivers. To get focused, sometimes, you cannot overlook those often-used rules of thumb like the "80/20 rule." When I re-launched Court Products, nearly 80% of the planned new company's sales were generated by only 20% of the inventory units stocked for the previous company. In addition, approximately 80% of the new company's sales would be driven by about 20% of the old company's underserved customers. Even before I bought the business from John, I should have made a stronger effort early on to learn the financial impact of our business plan. We had lost sight of the forest for the trees. That is, we were battling each order trying to make a buck to contribute to covering overhead costs but we had no strategy to actually focus on the best overall volume/margin mix.

Discounted Cash Flow (DCF) Analysis. The purest approach to valuing a company is to create a financial projection using as complete a picture as possible of all the expected inbound and outbound cash flows over a 5 to 8-year period. These cash flows are then discounted back to the present value. This is known as a discounted cash flow approach, or DCF from Finance 101. The last year is discounted into perpetuity (assuming the business is viewed as a going concern). As noted, there are many factors impacting cash flow which may be very difficult to confidently estimate and which could significantly impact the ultimate computation of value. Aside from these estimates, you will also need to select a discount rate to apply to those future cash flows and terminal value. Any finance textbook should be able to illustrate the basic requirements of a DCF analysis. Your own financial picture, how you will finance the purchase (that is, the portion of debt versus equity), and the general level of interest rates at the time of the purchase will also impact your discount rate assumption and DCF calculation.

The key point in performing a discounted cash flow analysis, whether in a business purchase or even a startup, is gaining comfort in the cash flow projections for the company YOU believe you will be able to build. Very clearly, should you personally be able to bring a value-enhancing incremental skill or competency to an existing business, you do not have to pay a seller for your value add. Rather, you should focus on the body of the seller's existing business which you would assume. What you add in terms of value is your upside alone.

KEY TAKEAWAYS

- Valuing a company requires a detailed discounted cash flow (DCF) analysis on the target opportunity

- Gain comparable business insights from online sources like bizbuysell.com

- If buying an existing company, don't pay for the incremental expertise and value you bring

Memo #10
To: Dan
Re: Situational Analysis

WHILE THE PREVIOUS STRATEGIC AND FINANCIAL analytical approaches can be scaled by breadth and depth to suit virtually any situation, sometimes you will encounter a more immediate or defined problem that requires solving. In my mind, I wasn't faced with starting a company completely from scratch, but maybe I should have approached it that way.

It was December of 1986 when I agreed to accept John's invitation to join Court Products. As mentioned, but worth reiterating here, I appreciate and value the marketing/sales requirement for any company (and any person). What I stumble on is the "schmoozing" portion of that salesmanship. I prefer my effort, actions and energy sell the concept. I consider myself a leader by example, not necessarily word. I just am not comfortable as a glib cocktail party guest with the innate ability to remember every child's name of every key business associate or contact.

My planned start date was January of 1987, following the holidays. Nevertheless, I was invited to the company holiday party. There was an air of anxiety as a result of the pending leadership change and financial stress of the company and I wasn't sure how the son-in-law coming aboard was going to be accepted. For that matter, I wasn't even sure how my joining was internally presented. Everybody was perfectly cordial and, given my wife was pregnant, we left the party a bit early. As I was walking out to the car, one lady on the team, Sunny, who was employee #1 for John dating back to the company's inception, yelled out the door "Don't worry, Todd, it's going to be great!" She clearly had read my face and somehow had the x-ray vision to see the churn in my stomach.

So, in early 1987 we began to dive in. Bill did his best to show me the ropes over his last two months. He was actually a good teacher. Nevertheless, the company continued to drift following his departure. This is one of those lessons about:

> "If you always do what you have always done, you will always get what you have always got."
> Attributed to: Jessie Potter in 1981, National Institute for Human Relationships

Said another way, the definition of insanity as attributed to several, including an ancient Chinese proverb, is:

> "Doing the same thing over and over again and expecting different results."

During this period, I had come to learn that John wasn't intimately involved in the daily business operations, he had essentially been owner of the racquetball clubs, the accompanying real estate and the financial capital behind Court Products. I did not view myself as his Chief Operating Officer, or COO. Rather, I felt more like an assistant manager executing the daily activities under John's direction. It was a period of just rolling up my sleeves and doing what needed to be done. As best as we knew how, Sunny and I co-ran the business with any big decisions, particularly those impacting us financially, taken to John for his concurrence. Our biggest salary, Bill, had been eliminated from the expense line and sales remained basically flat. In hindsight, this is one of those instances that I should have seized initiative and forced us to re-assess our approach. I could see personnel expense remained substantially out of balance with the overall level of sales and operational activity.

Then, we encountered another wrinkle. Just a few months later, Bill re-joined Court Products because his other opportunity did not work out from a personal/family perspective. He had approached John with a scripted turnaround plan which John thought worthy of an effort. John's directive, however, was that while Bill would lead the effort, the company was now ultimately destined for my control.

With a few additional hires and a return of Bill's salary, the expense line ballooned. A handful of months later, sales not materializing, we had to start cutting expenses again and that meant people. I became Bill's "voice" to direct others, something I profoundly regret, as it became painfully obvious that I was executing a good bit of the dirty work. Recall, you learn from good experiences and you learn from bad experiences. In Memo #28—Downsizing and Firing, we'll talk about how I could have handled the downsizing in a much more professional and personal manner.

Nearly a year later and despite a staff that had declined from 13 to seven, Bill's new plan faltered as well. John rightfully called a stop to acting as Court Products' forgiving bank. At this point, I even offered to leave to cut the expenses as I didn't see my role as critical for Bill's plan. John asked Bill how much he would pay to buy Court Products, but Bill said he couldn't or wouldn't want to buy it. In response, John basically pulled the plug and forced us to sit down and evaluate our options relative to the current day-to-day operating plan.

Here we were twice in three years re-evaluating strategies for survival. Chalk that up to a lost opportunity and a painful lesson learned. With a lack of true definition of my role, I definitely deferred too much to John and Bill's expertise and wound up singularly focused on executing whatever they directed. Even upon Bill's return and his revitalization plan, I just didn't challenge Bill's core premise which didn't really introduce any obvious change to spur increased sales and profit.

Rather than join an existing small business, you may likely start or buy your own business, so this experience is not apt to be one you will live out. Nevertheless, the lesson to take away is that the business you are running needs to foster a culture where your teammates can challenge your strategy and execution. The initial run of Court Products included a genial group of three "partners"—John, Bill and Sunny—that ran into a rapidly changing market. The internal challenge simply wasn't there until too late.

Deconstructing Problems and Opportunities. Now faced with the prospect of losing my own job, I approached John in mid-1990 and offered one last idea. I had reached the realization that I needed to spend my time fully analyzing the current broken business model to see if any aspect was worth saving. In order to do so, you have to deconstruct your business. That is, look at the pieces, whether from an operational, a customer segment or financial perspective. Which ones are working and why? Conversely, which ones are not and why? There is an analytical technique originating from Toyota Motor known as the "5 Whys." If you have a problem, you ask why does that specific problem occur. Based on the answer that typically begins with the word "because," you then ask "because why?" Keep iterating until that fifth "why" is answered and hopefully you have deconstructed the problem to its root cause. Then you can solve the problem more readily.

Whether a specific new opportunity, solving a problem, pursuing a particular growth opportunity, this diligence can and should be applied. Isolate the critical pieces and then use a technique like the "5 Whys." Don't forget to consider how the answers may impact you, your teammates and your core operation before deciding what changes may be necessitated.

My plan was to cut out all the slow moving high-end product as well as all the low margin product. As it were, these two subsets of inventory were focused on the waning racquetball club market. The focus going forward would be a renewed service-oriented push of proprietary product to the national not-for-profit clubs and organizations market. On the plus side, the regional and local outlets of these national clubs and organizations typically bought in bulk. As a draw-back to our current financial state, not-for-profits can be a cash flow challenge with respect to slow payment behavior. With this plan, we would just be carrying forward about 20% of our current business. So back to my design/build mantra, I now had a plan that I felt we could execute from the "strong bones" of Court Products existing operating infrastructure. Now at seven employees, I determined we would move forward with just myself and two others. Purchase agreement with John finished, shirtsleeves rolled up, the new Court Products began—and it was now all on me! I had now *chosen* this business.

KEY TAKEAWAYS

- Solving problems by determining root causes requires you to think "outside the box"

- Using Toyota's "5 Whys" can help deconstruct more narrowly defined, or situational, problems

File #4

Setting the Vision and Maintaining a Strategy

Memo #11

To: Dan

Re: Preparation for the Long Haul

IF YOU ARE A PARENT (or were ever a babysitter), think about that first note you left for your first babysitter. For some parents, it may have been a page long even though you were just popping over to the neighbors for a couple of hours. The vision—admittedly, probably not stated in writing at the top although heavily implied and inferred— was "ensure the baby is OK." There were probably a series of rather detailed "steps" to assure a successful outcome over the next two hours: phone number for any question/problem/emergency (no matter how trivial); feeding directions accompanied by a visual tour of the fridge; diaper changing; bedtime ritual; etc., etc. There was no doubt that babysitter had a clear view of your vision and the strategies you intended for them to execute!

From a different perspective, in the large corporate arena, there is something called an "elevator speech Yes, these can happen in small business as well, but it may be a walk in from the parking lot and hopefully everyone already knows each other rather well. In any case, the elevator speech is intended to be that 30 to 45 second statement you could offer to a senior executive to express who you are, what you do and how well you do it. It's your personal vision statement and how you are going about executing upon it. For the entrepreneur, think about how you would articulate your vision and strategy to someone asking you what you do for a living at your next neighborhood block party. Of course, they won't ask in those terms, but they may very well ask "what makes a company like yours successful and how are you better than the competition?" Bottom line, you have quite likely dictated a vision and strategy before for some important endeavor (protecting your newborn) or for some other perfectly normal communication.

So, for your company, set a vision that is understood and shared by all (preferably written for all to see). Have it clearly and concisely state that this is who we are. This is what we do. This is what makes us different from the competition and therefore better. These are our guiding principles, the foundation of all our decisions.

A critical aspect of setting out the vision and strategy for your team is preparation for handling any manner of crises—an inevitable encounter. A crisis may come in varying degrees; it could be a physical event at a plant such as fire or it could be an extended absence of a key teammate. It could even be your own extended absence. Then, when that next crisis hits, it will be easier to fall back on these principles to resolve difficult decisions. If you have also coached your team on the critical steps to run the business successfully, your ability to withstand a large setback is enhanced if your team understands the effort required when a crisis occurs. Setting a well-communicated vision and supporting strategy is not just about daily execution, it's about gaining a competitive advantage that will drive your company's success.

KEY TAKEAWAYS

- Vision and strategy are not just about executing for the day to day, it's about gaining a long-term competitive edge

- A well-articulated and communicated vision and strategy is an insurance policy if your company hits a crisis

- Don't just write a vision and strategy down; communicate them, live them as a team

Memo #12
To: Dan
Re: The Vision

MY DAY 1 EXPERIENCE AT THE *"NEW"* COURT PRODUCTS was that of a forced turnaround. We had run the numbers and the status quo was out. The business required focus on who managed, how they managed, what we sold, to whom and how.

Setting a vision sounds simple in words, but in practice it involves an iterative effort of articulating ideals, testing their validity, and honest analysis to pivot when dead ends or dark corners are encountered. Further, once you embark on your pursuit of this vision, your planned financial and operational results may not manifest themselves immediately. Your pursuit may require some tactical, or strategic, revamping and new direction.

Looking back over the last thirty years, there is no question that the re-evaluation of our industry, figuring out where we fit in at that point in time, how we were going to position ourselves and what we were going to focus upon turned out to create a fulfilling career for me and an economic livelihood for my team and family. Nevertheless, as you spend time developing that vision and testing it within the knowledge set of your current market environment, the likelihood is that it may take a few years before you are able to realize whether the right path was followed or success was attained. Patience during your ramp-up is critical, you can't rush through these important early stages of building a quality business by cutting corners. And perhaps most critical of all, as the years progress, you must keep a pulse on your industry and the happenings within your own walls and be prepared to strategically react in order to stay aligned to your vision.

Articulating the Vision. Court Products does not have a company slogan or a written set of core principles developed by an expensive image consultant. Quite frankly, maybe we should be more formal about our vision and supporting principles—particularly as we begin a transition to another generation. Nobody knows our business better, we can create our own without the expensive consultant. There is nothing hokey about ensuring your team is absolutely certain of what you deem essential to driving the company's success. And, it does not matter whether that team can be counted all on one hand or multiples thereof. Setting your company's vision is not an organizational exercise for just you, it is a pathway to ensuring your business culture engenders behavior that systemically supports attainment of that vision. The implementation of your vision through your business strategies provides the systematic discipline to achieve the vision.

Abraham Lincoln stated:

> "Determine that the thing can and shall be done and then we shall find the way."

Your vision is that "thing" supported by your principles and core values. Finding the way is all about your strategic initiatives. Think of your vision as the top of a pyramid. It sits above all but, importantly, is supported by a set of defining principles or core values and a set of critical strategic initiatives.

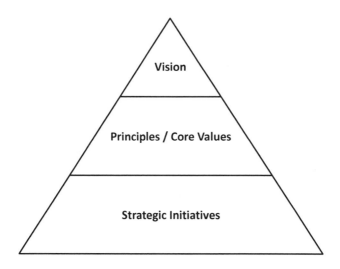

There are a couple of important supporting considerations when you think about establishing your vision for your company. First, seek that lofty goal that inspires everyday excellence and, second, ensure your actual product or service aligns to your vision? For example, Nike seeks "to bring inspiration and innovation to every athlete in the world." The inspiration and innovation is part of the vision and incorporating the athlete ties directly to their product line. Likewise, Starbucks seeks "to inspire and nurture the human spirit—one person, one cup and one neighborhood at a time."

Another important consideration, particularly for a small business, is the actual name you stencil on the door. Does it align to your vision, what does it convey, how does it relate to your product or service offering, how will the vast majority of your customers perceive it? It can definitely become a helpful driver of positive name recognition, but it can also create some unintended headaches. Think of a hypothetical company, Body Grafix. What does it do? Tattoos, automobile exterior stenciling, t-shirts? Not unlike naming your child, this can become a very nuanced—but important—effort when launching your company. We thought about a re-branding when we re-launched Court Products. Even Court Products has received requests for gavels and stenographic machines! In the end, we opted to maintain the name given our somewhat precarious condition so as to provide confidence to vendors and not plant the notion of a perceived ownership and management change. Weighing the plusses and minuses is an important exercise in the naming and branding element of setting your vision.

I have always stressed "service"—we essentially sell nothing but a service despite "product" being the visual flow. We know our customers can buy most of the items we sell from any number of competitors. Thus, it comes down to the quality of our service that will keep them coming back time and time again. I stress this service vision in every interview with prospective employees and it is a staple of our weekly team meetings, particularly when new catalogues are mailed or the website updated. The message is, which I am sure each teammate can recite, "remember, this product offering isn't all we sell, we sell *service!*" As the years have progressed, the team has very effectively engrained this behavior into their routine as our growth has largely come from selling more styles of essentially the same product lines to essentially the same customer types. Thus, while our offering and our target customer base have both expanded, the core of what we do has not changed substantially in thirty years. Hence, our vision of a concerted focus on service remains entirely appropriate today.

This focus on service also drives our efforts around the design and layout of our core marketing tools, the catalogue and website. We want to ensure a user-friendly experience, not necessarily one that is going to win a designer award. User-friendly and great service are synonymous in my view. User-friendly to us is the ability to efficiently peruse a catalogue or website, find what you need or have an idea spark ignited, easily basket your selections, transition to checkout with critical quantity, color, size choices summarized and then execute the order online or via call-in.

From personal experience, I am sure you have been online for certain sites where you struggle to reach closure or checkout and the angst builds quickly. Worse, you execute an order based on some online or catalogue representation and it just doesn't meet your expectations upon arrival. We have had to dial back some catalogue designers in favor of greater simplicity. We'd rather our client can readily see what they actually expect than inflicting a bit of harm to a catalogue designer's artistic pride. While online orders are making a substantial inroad to those from our original hard-copy catalogue approach, the final test is the actual physical view and touch of that product upon delivery. Online marketing, despite the technology to provide up-close or magnified viewing, is not immune from displaying pictures that may not square with a customer's hands-on expectations. We do get positive feedback from our customers on ease of navigation, quick ship-to-order cycles and ready access to our sales team for questions—it is all part of that bundled service focus.

Our #1 goal then is providing customers a pleasant experience when talking to our team and projecting a positive attitude about delivering exactly what the customers are seeking. Without this primary focus, how else would we be able to facilitate repeat business. Our business model could not survive a "one and done" sales model. In fact, few small businesses can.

For Court Products, excellent service is the vision; that is, delivering a positive customer experience, one that warrants repeat visits. In some respects, you might argue that any business must focus on service first. It is key, but think of a manufacturer that is able to deliver the wonder-widget on time, every time, but its quality is suffering badly. It doesn't matter if that part is where it needs to be when it needs to be; if it doesn't work, it isn't worth anything. For other businesses, say a small-town pharmacist, control procedures to ensure sensitive medications are handled, tracked, dispensed according to strict guidelines are a must. You might be great at home delivery in a pinch to relieve that person's ailment, but if a state regulatory agency put you out of business for an inability to safely manage controlled medications, you might be out of business quickly. Each business has its nerve center, the trick is finding what that critical element may be. From there, you may have some ancillary aspects of the business that pull together to form a complete picture of your vision. As noted, the manufacturer must focus on quality, but customer service is right behind. The small-town pharmacist must focus on safety and controls, but customer service is also a tight second.

Supporting Principles/Core Values. Within the realm of high quality service as a vision, there are some important sub-plots. Specifically, it's important to identify some of the supporting principles that form the foundation for your business' vision.

Whether family, friends or business partners, most people would describe me as a pretty laid back, low key, approachable personality. My competitive fires burn at the right times, I don't have to wear them on my sleeve. Early on, I decided that if I were going to own and run my own business, then I wanted it to be a fun place to come to work. Yes, I get they call it "work" for a reason, but I didn't want an employee to feel it was a drag to come in each day. Thus, one supporting principle to my vision was setting a positive tone for the Court Products' environment. It was going to be a fun place to come to work, a relaxed atmosphere where the goal was that everyone felt comfortable with everyone else. A place where you knew your teammates and respect was a given. Since Court Products must sell "service" to effectively succeed within our target market, my hope was this approach would translate to the voices our customers heard when we answered our phones and the efforts we expended on delivering each order. Finding similarly-minded teammates, then, became integral to that supporting principle.

Another of our supporting principles is beginning each relationship from a position of trust. Like any business where human error is a possibility, distribution businesses will encounter shipment mistakes. If a customer calls to report they were shorted on an order, regardless of what our paperwork, inventory and ship weight might indicate, we would likely swallow our pride and resolve the customer's problem. You can't run a business questioning the honesty of all your customers, there has to be a level of trust. Of course, if these particular errors persist across the customer base, it is a yellow flag to review your internal operational controls. If it is focused around a couple of specific customers, maybe an eventual challenge is in order. Frankly, sometimes a customer may need awareness their own receiving department is in desperate need of straightening out.

We'll talk a bit later in Memo #17 (Driving Sales, Managing Costs) about our principle of ethical bidding when vendors vie for our business. Essentially, we drive toward fair, transparent relationships. Sounds easy, but you really have to consistently execute on such a principle for some time before you see that relationship reciprocity develop. Similar to our customers that may call with an erroneous shipment or a last-minute need, we may have the same situation with a supplier. Just as we view "outbound" quality service as our vision to success, we do expect that our vendors will treat us with equal respect. In order to deliver that high-quality service component to our customers, we rely on our vendors to be part of our vision. Understanding the linkages in your business that allow you to fully execute your vision is important to driving the cooperation you need throughout your supply, execution and delivery chain.

The sign over the Court Products door should then read:

Court Products, Inc.
Where Great Customer Service Matters

- Is a fun place to work
- Values trusting partnerships
- Creates fair, transparent relationships

Maintaining the Vision. Once you have articulated your vision, how do you ensure you maintain the straight and narrow? Or is that even essential if your business environment is rapidly changing? One might argue that if you have to change your vision, perhaps you have actually started a new business. This was my experience taking over Court Products and discontinuing the racquetball business. You may have to fine tune elements of your vision over time, but a wholesale change in the core of that vision and supporting principles does insinuate a new venture or a significant change in your industry environment. Technology driven businesses are probably those most susceptible to a completely new paradigm causing a wholesale re-assessment of a company's vision.

What is very common, however, are off-shoots of your core business. Exploring avenues for additional growth may prompt you to expand your product or service offering to add-ons that would effectively flourish because they share the same business fundamentals as your core business. Just as ensuring you periodically re-visit the vision and principles supporting your core business, you need to be prepared to test any new growth opportunity so as to avoid killing that goose that laid the golden egg. Placing a bet on a new venture that risks the livelihood of the core business isn't just a financial question. You must be prepared to challenge yourself on time and resource commitments taken away from the core business.

At Court Products, each time we try to think of methods to expand the business, we first re-visit what has brought us to this point in our company history and what it is we do best. Our starting point is typically to build on the company infrastructure in place in order to manage the incremental costs that come with such an expansion plan. That is: a quality service team, custom designs, warehouse capacity and an effective shipping operation, an 800 number and catalogue production/online experience, etc. If we cannot leverage what we do best, then we really challenge ourselves as to whether adding a second line of business dependent on something we can do "second best" is going to be good enough to achieve success.

We certainly have not tried to become a completely different company overnight, nor would we risk the core business for a venture with which we would have no experience. For any new business line, you should re-evaluate those same aspects discussed in File #2 (Is Small Business Right for You?) and #3 (Getting Started) when you completed your personal and business analysis. What is the environment, how will you fit in, who will be your vendors and customers, etc. For our distribution business, we naturally would launch from some of our core strengths and infrastructure. We wouldn't branch into retail from there, it would just be too long a leap.

One area many businesses often look toward for expansion is vertical integration. That is, moving up or down the food chain of their industry model. This, too, can be fraught with peril even though the industry lineage and knowledge exists. The technical and service skills at different stages of production for a product or service, as well as their delivery model, can require vastly different proficiencies. You must carefully pencil out the impact a vertical expansion step will have on your business. Critically, it shouldn't be something that forces your company to become something it is not. With careful planning, such an expansion may not be all bad if you are truly looking to diversify and grow. If what you become, however, cannot be managed effectively by who you inherently are, then problems may arise very quickly.

As an example, in my business a vertical step could be bringing our own t-shirt brand in-house. That industry-aligned step would, however, turn us into a manufacturer and a volume driven shop—which strays quite a distance from a service-oriented distributor. The financial impact of buying the machinery, adding more warehouse space and building a larger workforce would in no way create sufficient savings on the volumes we move even accounting for greater inventory control and enhanced delivery to customers. If we attempted to average down those increased costs, we would have to be cutting and sewing during at least two shifts and would end up completely engulfed in finding new customer markets. It just isn't where our knowledge and experience lie. Vertical integration seems like a natural extension in a market you might know, but it can very easily turn your company into something it is not.

Outside vertical integration, product extension is also a common approach to growth. We often thought it would be great if we were able to develop our own proprietary line of tee shirt designs. The idea being that it would require nearly identical operational execution through the same supply chain. The new line would provide us freedom of design, no restrictions from a national governing club or organization. It would also allow us to sell at retail prices versus our current wholesale market, thereby increasing our margins and generating a satisfying feeling of accomplishment. We settled on, Alpine Way, an outdoor active theme for hikers, mountain bikers, etc. since this mirrored our personal interests and, again, operationally piggy-backed the current business. Our current customers have members that are the outdoor/recreation/leisure people we envisioned. And, since we held ourselves in that class and liked our designs and product choices, we were hopeful others would, too.

Well, we missed something in our customer analysis and thus whiffed on the appropriate target market. Our existing national clubs and organizations order mainly for their current programs and indoor facilities. While our new line sported recreation and leisure designs, they just didn't fit with core indoor and outdoor programs our customers offered. Court Products' customer buyers were buying for their programs, not for their members' personal interests. The experience served as an important reminder to reinforce the notion of knowing your market and its consumption behavior and requirements. Attempting to go direct to the individual buyer would cause us to stray from our vision. While our Alpine Way business was a well-designed quality retail product, there wasn't going to be a substantive quality customer service component upon which we could capitalize.

In a similar version of expansion, we were approached by a few branches of one not-for-profit organization to offer access to our products directly to their members. The idea was to create a virtual retail store for the organizations' branches so they would not have to staff it, purchase inventory, and process payments. This was a market we had often discussed and thought the opportunity to tap a higher margin segment would be welcome. We attended their national industry conference of market directors as a potential vendor, built a separate website and produced sales flyers. Then launched. Then flopped. We weren't given access to the real customer in this transaction. We couldn't contact them directly to advertise the program as we were not able to gain member lists. It was left to the branch's discretion how it was communicated and that essentially was: "Here's a website if you have interest."

Bottom line, our expertise is business to business, not retail. This foray into a retail market where we were not given the ability to create any direct customer experience broke the linkage to our vision.

We learned a lesson that we have to control our market and ours is not a model that allows us to "sub-contract" our key focus—providing quality service.

- Settling on a vision is an iterative effort of articulating ideals and testing their validity

- A vision centers around what is essential to drive your company's success; it's the nerve center

- As your industry and business change, maintaining alignment to a vision focuses the company on what and how to adapt

- Setting a vision is not a one-time exercise, it is a method of forming a business culture

- Consider supporting principles or core values as a means to clarify your vision

- Test your growth opportunities for alignment to your company's vision

Memo #13
To: Dan
Re: The Strategy

NOW THAT YOU HAVE ESTABLISHED A VISION and perhaps some supporting principles, you need to have a plan to execute. Articulating your strategic approaches to core aspects of your business can help avoid breakdowns of process as you progress toward fulfilling your vision for your company. A strategy can provide you and your team a more tangible and operational roadmap to realizing your vision and achieving your goals. Just like a vision, it is worth articulating on paper what those strategies are that will drive your business. As Ben Franklin stated:

"By failing to prepare, you are preparing to fail."

Today, you often see the quote specifically modified for business teams: Failing to plan is planning to fail.

Identify the core activities and initiatives that are the foundational building blocks of delivering your product or service, stipulate timing or cycles and assign responsibilities. The timing and cycles shouldn't all be identical and occurring within one "big bang" week. Otherwise, you will compromise effectiveness. A strategic plan should instill a model of discipline that allows the company to track toward its goals. Think of these strategies as an operational insurance policy. Should you personally require an unanticipated extended leave of absence, how well would your team be able to step in and execute in order to preserve smooth working order? Importantly, these strategic initiatives should not be confused with tactical or operational duties or process guides for job tasks.

Strategic Plan Example. At Court Products, high quality service is the vision. In order to deliver on that, we have to ensure we are consistently executing to plan on our pre-determined critical strategic steps. From this strategic point of view, we have a few key areas of focus. First, is the process around the annual catalogue. You can understand there are many tactical aspects to its production and distribution, but that highlights the difference between strategic plans and tactical or operational procedures. Strategically, we need to ensure we initiate an annual production process, supplemented by seasonal flyers, to hit our customers' buying cycles in order to enhance attainment of our annual sales goals.

Increasingly today, given the web-based buying trends of our customers, we ensure we complete a parallel review of our website including a comprehensive run through of product displays, checkout and test orders. This ensures the front-end marketing from the website operationally fits into our order processing, warehouse fulfillment and shipping and receivables collection processes. It also allows us to test how well we are informing our customers about our commitment to providing prompt delivery, flexible ordering quantities and appropriate credit limits supplemented by access to competitive prices including quantity discounts and monthly specials. The catalogue and the website are the tangible results of this strategic effort, but there are important operational aspects to our sales strategy that also require periodic review to ensure the competitiveness of the overall effort.

A corollary to the above customer-focused strategy is a review of our vendors to ensure they 1) offer the product we intend to advertise and 2) can produce the quality finished product we envision. You will undoubtedly have multiple vendors, they will not all be able to meet every one of your product, quantity, time, and quality needs. As such, it is very important to periodically assess whether you have become aligned to some vendors that are potentially inhibiting your ability to deliver quality product and service to your customers.

In no particular order of importance, our second key strategy is to evaluate the alignment of our team to the tasks and responsibilities required to deliver for our customers. Regardless of seniority, we can't afford to place someone in a sales role if they just don't have the appropriate personality (recall Memo #4—Is Your Personality the Right Fit?). Our employee role assignment strategy is to match each person's skills to the most appropriate roles and responsibilities that will contribute to the greater good of the company. Again, you can see there are many tactical steps (i.e. annual performance reviews and appraisals) we have to take to analyze and execute this strategy. We have been fortunate that our team has been reasonably stable over the years, but it has not kept us from testing ourselves to ensure we are each effectively aligned in the most optimal way.

A third element of our strategy for ensuring a positive customer experience is the ability to deliver the order accurately and timely. We do periodically test our production and warehouse to ensure the stocking of product and the flow of packaged orders is working its way to customers as efficiently as possible. It isn't rocket science, but if we can do things to minimize mistakes and expedite shipments, we are delivering on our vision. Further, depending on the ebb and flow of business, we may have different people stepping up to provide surge capacity. It is important that we then have a system we all understand and can execute within.

Our fourth strategic review comes around our computer and technology capabilities. Like the rest of society, our customers are driving toward paperless recordkeeping. We must keep pace to their approach or we could lose sales opportunities. While there is a cost to maintain and sometimes upgrade our systems, we have also enjoyed savings in our own administrative processing and mailing costs for billing. Having been the victim of a computer hacking incident, we hired a technology consultant. Today, that consultant provides us updates not only on security, but also on applicable software options. Given the pace of technological change, this has become part of our strategic review.

The fifth item on our strategic agenda is the development of an annual financial plan or budget. If we have no ability to hold ourselves accountable, we risk running off plan and placing the entire company at risk of failure. For Court Products, it is a check and balance on how well our catalogue and web offering are meeting market demands. Budgeting for any company is a must. Inevitably, there will be unforeseen developments that pop up during the year that will challenge the ability to stay on plan or, hopefully, create welcome revenue and profit surprises.

There are a couple aspects of budgeting that are worth highlighting. First is the ability to create financial and operational benchmarks that measure your sales progress, cost control and production efficiency. Using the data your company generates, create thoughtful informational benchmarks combining two pieces of data. For instance, sales and employee counts are two pieces of data. Sales per employee provides a measure of your production efficiency. Secondly, budgeting allows for businesses to plan for larger one-off expenditures. If you are a manufacturer and need to expand capacity, where will you access the capital? Maybe you need to determine some reserve to set aside each year in order to save up for such an expenditure or you need to use your budget to demonstrate to a banker you can repay a loan of a certain amount.

For many similar companies to Court Products where we target long customer lists with print or electronic media, we have a periodic strategic initiative to scrub the accuracy of our database. If we are sending out paper catalogues by mail to hundreds of people no longer working in those roles, even if they land in the right building, they could end up in the trash before getting out of the mail room. This becomes a waste of print and postage for us, not to mention our environmental impact due to unused paper catalogues. E-mail lists are less costly to maintain, but are important to scrub for accuracy to ensure your marketing is making it to an actual buyer. If we get an error on delivery, at least we know we have to follow up to gain a new address for a new buyer at our existing customer.

Finally, none of these strategies, nor the execution of the tactical roles and responsibilities, will be effective without a clear and transparent communication regimen. In a small business, people are often working as interchangeable parts to the whole of the company. If we aren't communicating, doubling up of the same effort or, worse yet, assuming something was done and creating a gap in customer service, can all be the result. To avoid this, our weekly team meeting is an opportunity to ensure an open airing of what might be coming around the next corner, what is working well, what requires attention and who needs to be brought up to speed on what.

Testing Your Strategies' Validity. Strategies will require adjustments over time as your business environment changes; the mailing lists being just one issue. Just as you went through an initial business evaluation (Memo #8—Strategic Analysis) on your chosen opportunity, intuitively, you should update the same exercise every couple of years or following any major impact to your company's market environment. As stated, we are increasingly finding that our online communication is gaining greater acceptance than the original cornerstone physical catalogue. It is not likely we could pinpoint what year this began nor the precise annual impact, thus that reinforces the need to have a set periodic strategic review. It is natural for any business to have to pivot on strategy, thus it requires open eyes and open minds to identify change and accept change. Court Products has been spending much more time evaluating the mix of sales from the web versus our catalogue. We need to be prepared to adapt to our relative investment of production on each. Secondarily, we have to ensure we have the right people with the right technical skills to help us evolve our sales model to the web, Facebook, and other social media channels.

Sometimes, evolutions in the market for your product or service may influence changes in your company's strategies and operating initiatives. Communication strategies and approaches, like every other aspect of your business, also must align and adjust to these changes. Focusing on knowing your customer is critical, but "knowing" is far more than simply understanding their buying motivation. It is also about understanding how to best communicate and educate your customer about evolutions in your industry, product, service or technology. Adapting your product or service without adjusting your communications can result in a painful lesson.

When performance/breathable apparel (i.e. CoolMax) hit the market around 2007, the marketing and advertising of manufacturers like Nike, UnderArmour, etc. jumped out front to educate the consumer far quicker than our capability to do so. The result was that we had our customers looking for the performance/breathable product from us which created a bit of a race with the competition to address our customers' demand. We thought we had a solid offering to address this new development. Bearing in mind our value-add is taking a manufacturer's product and custom printing a range of club or organizational requirements, we worked with our vendors on addressing the new craze.

First, a slight digression and explanation. Sublimation is a form of printing wherein the fabric of the original piece of apparel has die applied. Contrast this with a silk-screening approach which applies a full new layer of plastisol ink. Plastisol ink can leave a non-breathable print that dries with a stiff, rougher feel on the garment. The new breathable fabrics were designed to be lightweight and moisture wicking. Thus, silk-screening actually completely reverses the technology by trapping in heat and moisture in addition to adding weight.

Court Products offered two designs of a particular performance product and, owing to the sublimation process, we had to buy a minimum of 500 of each. The quantity was driven by the desire to stay competitive and keep the costs down on this new sublimation process, which is more expensive than silk-screening. In our catalogue, we offered both the traditional silk-screened product as well as our new, improved, bolder dynamic sublimation design. It was the same underlying product with both printing approaches. The sublimation price, however, was nearly twice that of the silk-screened price. Needless to say, without the ability to actually touch and feel a product in our catalogue, our customers thought saving money for their constituents was the best way to go. We ended up eating many of the higher-priced sublimation-printed product. While not a crippling financial loss, we learned a valuable lesson in strategically introducing new product—educate the customer!

Monitoring the Strategic Plan. Monitoring the critical elements of your strategic plan requires both an upfront and ongoing commitment. The upfront investment requires you to establish the key performance indicators (some refer to them as KPIs) that can quantitatively measure your progress and adherence to plan. These KPIs should have an established review cycle by the people or teams held responsible.

The financial statements and reports detailing business activity will naturally provide a ready source of KPIs. That said, it may be necessary to get creative at tracking other important benchmarks. You cannot readily see on an income statement the percentage of teammate appraisals completed or the number of returns of a particular product or hits on your website. Think as well about sales trends. If you sold 100 of a product, did you sell twenty lots of five each or one sale of the entire 100? Such information will greatly inform your operating strategies. Your annual budget and financial planning strategy is a good launch point to select your financial KPIs to monitor for the coming year.

One caveat of KPIs in a small business environment is not to go overboard and measure everything. Focus on what you can readily measure via your incoming data. Think about what information that data can tell you about your business. Is that information something that is material to your company's success? Does it help measure progress toward your goals? Can it help you steer clear of impending problems? Have you launched a new business initiative that requires an acceleration of data gathering and monitoring? The scope, frequency and one-off requirements for data should be driven by the nature of your business, there is no standard template.

For those of you that were business majors in school, you are very likely familiar with Peter Drucker, one of the most accomplished thinkers and authors of business management. One of Drucker's famous mantras was:

"If you can't measure it, you can't improve it."

We worked with our accountant early on to establish some of the financial metric reporting that would help us keep a finger on the pulse of our operations. Importantly, don't get trapped in just following sales and income measures. An uncontrolled cost structure is the greatest evil of an otherwise good business idea. KPIs focused around your critical costs—whether it be materials, maintenance or employees—are an absolute must. As mentioned, taking two data points together and creating one piece of information is also extremely insightful. Calculating your cost per unit of production, sales per employee or any number of ratio driven relative measures can help you manage your company's productivity. Finally, a data point is only a data point, not information. You will need to be committed to collecting these data points so that you can see what information they collectively provide you over some measure of time.

In our distribution business, we have a sharp focus on inventory. We track on-hand, customer-committed and vendor-ordered quantities of our SKUs relative to sales to help ensure against stock-outs or bloated inventory. The relative measure to overall sales provides us a strong running picture of what is selling and what is not. We run the numbers on a portion of inventory everyday so that by every week's end, we have covered it all. With data like this, we can figure out the cost of a product's warehouse space, catalog space, inventory turn and weigh that against its sales volume and margin. This information then tells us whether or not, on a relative basis, the product should be continued. Taking it a step further, that helps us focus on getting the customer the product they most value—that enhances our ability to deliver high quality customer service.

In general, the sales, inventory and shipping cost data are all for the team's consumption. There are some KPIs a small business owner may wish to monitor privately. Not surprisingly, most of that would deal with employee related costs and performance. There are other administrative and operating costs as well that your team generally does not require to effectively carry out their responsibilities. Just because these data points are not being prepared for team consumption, however, you must maintain the review discipline to watch for critical information on cost management.

Make Time for Strategy Setting and Review. Big corporations are famous for their annual "executive retreats" where presumably they affirm their vision and evaluate their current strategies and refine them with fresh perspectives freed by the fresh air consumed during rounds of golf. Why can't you do the same? Seriously, if you need to provide a booster to the process, can you convince your team to take a day (maybe a Saturday if the office must be open) filled with the promise of a fun team-building outing and dinner? The investment would likely pay handsome returns over time.

Strategy review, however, is more than an annual ceremonial process. Our annual catalogue process and website review establishes a very visible and programmatic launch point to review our sales process and effectiveness. It provides an opportunity to evaluate the successes and the factors that contributed to each. Similarly, we take time to look at the challenges we encountered and diagnose those causes. For such an impactful element of our business, we must provide an appropriate commitment of time and resource in preparing to monitor and adapt our catalogue and website success (or failure) to the evolution of our business environment. Our strategic review does not stop at mailing or re-launch, we systematically monitor progress on what is working and what is not and challenge ourselves whether we stuck to what we know best or we ventured into a completely foreign arena. Knowing the strategies critical to implementing your business' vision and investing time for formal periodic reviews can make or break your financial success.

The quality of your strategy setting and review will only be as good as the inputs you use. It is absolutely critical to have the right team players at the table evaluating these issues so that you understand the impact of any changes in direction. Further, there are no better people to provide a factual view of those input factors than the people executing on the current approach. If we learn of procedures that don't work well, we address them to improve efficiency or evaluate the team skills to possibly re-distribute responsibilities.

The risk of holding to a systematic annual review of your key strategies is that you risk having critical inputs fall through the cracks during the year. It is important during the daily, weekly, monthly communication routines that observations are voiced (and HEARD) and tracked to ensure a complete record of inputs is brought to the table. Hearing directly from the front lines and the feedback they receive from customers and vendors about all aspects of your product or service offering is invaluable. It is where your vision's rubber meets the road!

One risk in a small business, however, is the boss may have launched the business with a very visible coronation. In Monarchies, what the King/Queen says, goes. Consider, however, the number of voices in a small business that can truly impact your success or failure. If you silence just one of seven, you have just cut out nearly 15% of your feedback loop. There is no question that the ultimate decisions are yours, it is your company. Nevertheless, the small business owner must be careful to listen, learn and—where possible—incorporate the team's input into those decisions. You can't be with each customer and each vendor at every touchpoint, so value the feedback and distill any emotion that may be over-dramatizing the news you hear. It is important they see their input as making a difference, otherwise, you will stifle further contributions and your business will suffer as the team becomes reluctant to participate.

As an example, the substantial effort athletic and leisure apparel manufacturers have invested in women's styling and design over the past few decades is highly evident. When I started out, basically all t-shirts were men's t-shirts. I have made a point of maintaining my strong knowledge of what products are on offer in the market. Nevertheless, the women on my teams have had an equally strong contribution to insights on these evolving trends and, subsequently, on our product offering. Receiving firsthand feedback from my team—and even their spouses—whether through customer discussions or personal experience is invaluable. Individually, I just can't appreciate the range of styling, color or fit preferences across our vast customer base. In a small business, you have to leverage your team as a key "market perception detector" because you just can't be expected to see or experience it all.

Gaining External Perspective. In File #7 (Chief Administrative Officer) we will discuss more about the use of external professionals and advisors, however, it is worth a mention here as well. Setting strategy sets the framework for how you and the team will execute the daily tactical roles and responsibilities. If you are hung up and uncertain how to interpret the impact to your business of certain elements in the business environment, seek the viewpoints of others. Reach out to those you know and trust as a sounding board. The connection need not be an elaborate, scripted gathering, consider one-off meetings or lunches. And if your first contact is unable to help, perhaps they will help connect you to the right person in their network that can provide advice and counsel.

I did have a bit of a luxury when we re-launched Court Products as John was able to act as an onsite chairman emeritus. He had begun this business twelve years prior and willingly helped as an expert sounding board and advice provider. His involvement serving on various bank and community boards established a solid base of connections that provided entry to a network of subject matter experts I did not have. Any small business owner will begin to develop their own network through the use of outside experts like accountants, attorneys, employment agencies, etc. There is no better time to develop that network than Day 1! LinkedIn or local business groups like the Rotary Club can serve as a helpful beginning.

KEY TAKEAWAYS

- A strategy is a tangible and operational roadmap to executing toward your vision

- Identify and articulate the core initiatives that are building blocks to delivering for your customer

- Strategies may need to change, or pivot, to respond to a changing market; but they should preserve alignment to your vision

- Evaluate your business results against your strategies; errors or missed opportunities may require a change of course

- Monitor your execution of strategy by identifying key performance indicators to track over time relative to expectations

- Periodic strategic reviews require setting aside time— away from daily operational activities

- Don't overlook the value of additional viewpoints from your team, your vendors, your customers and even external professionals

Memo #14
To: Dan
Re: **Crisis Management**

A FOCUSED VISION with a carefully planned supporting strategy can help protect the core of your business through a crisis. Following through on the steps above provides your team the communication and understanding they need to focus on the required tasks to run your business. It will provide them understanding of your desire to help drive the creation of a profitable company that supports their own stable job opportunities. But, as the saying goes, "the best laid plans . . .."

There are some crises that might require you to develop a sub-strategy to effectively deal with them in a manner that walls off any negative impact to the core business. When we re-launched Court Products, the not-for-profit clubs and organizations business was only 20% of the former entity. Effectively, we created a separate "run off" or discontinued business line for the remaining 80% and placed all the racquetball-related assets within it. This required a host of critical actions including separating everything from our inventory to our financial books. Customer and vendor discussions and interactions required careful thought and dialogue so as not to create a market panic about whether we were going out of business. Crises tend to impact the team, as well; and, we were not immune. If clear communication is important to run your business on a normal day, think what it takes when the tornado has kicked up all sorts of debris to swirl about everyone's head. People need to know not only what to do, but also where they stand and how they fit in. You may not be able to provide this clarity while in the eye, but you must communicate as best you can.

It is hard to predict the type of crisis your company may one day face. Dan's decision to stay with the company has now relieved the pressure around leadership were something to happen to me. I can't imagine how my wife would have stepped in to find someone to run our company had something happened to me. It is absolutely essential that you, your family and some of your key professional advisors like accountants, lawyers and estate or financial planners know of your plan for such an instance. There are retired executives available as crisis managers. With a well-articulated strategic plan, you may very well enhance their ability to maintain your business' value.

Financial setbacks and prolonged cash drains can also be difficult to predict, but they frequently happen to small businesses. Knowing what it might take and how much additional capital you can access from outside investors, bankers or other personal sources of savings or insurance is worth exploring as a precaution during personal crises or business slowdowns.

KEY TAKEAWAYS

- A well-communicated set of key strategic initiatives supporting your company's vision establishes a strong roadmap for all to follow in the event of a crisis

- In the absence of the founder, an outside executive hire would be far better prepared to maintain the business' value with a clearly articulated strategic plan

File #5

Running the Business Operations

Memo #15
To: Dan
Re: Getting Focused

WHEN I WAS WORKING IN THE POOL BUSINESS, visiting job sites was at the top of the list of my favorite things to do. What clearly struck me at first glance was the obvious big hole in the ground that would eventually become a gleaming facility that one day might host championship competitions. In fact, I went on one trip to a national testing lab where we were developing a new product to roll out nationally with a hoped-for adoption into the next Olympic venue. Talk about visually setting your sights on the business. It is very energizing to witness physical progress, but it is also critical to understand how to manage getting to that finished product.

Importantly, moving your business from inception to realizing some of those dreams does take a level of patience. You must have a willingness to press on beyond some of the inevitable starting bumps; don't bail out too soon as stability out of the box is by no means normal. To get beyond that challenging period, it will require your diligent focus across many business processes.

In small business, you really need to run the business by immersing yourself in all facets of it. Not all aspects will be as energizing as producing a product destined for the Olympics, but all are critical to ensuring all the gears are well-oiled. No pun intended there, but a manufacturer that doesn't maintain the plant and equipment may quickly learn it's not only the gears that are gummed up.

As I learned from my early days when Court Products struggled, cash flow is the focus. For all those business majors, your accounting classes taught you that very early on. For those non-business majors, as you line up capital to support your endeavor, you quickly discover the questions directed to you by bankers and other investors are all focused on the ability to generate sustainable cash flow to support ongoing operations, growth capital, loan repayments and dividends.

Certainly, there are drivers of cash flow that one normally associates with running their finger down the Income Statement or the Balance Sheet. Thus, a discussion about running the business and associated management routines can also be organized around a tour through the financial statements. We'll talk about some of those decisions that have big impacts, but watching that cash balance is where it all begins.

KEY TAKEAWAYS

- You must have intimate knowledge of what it takes to get your company to deliver a finished product or service

- Think of how to run your business by focusing on critical elements of your financial statements, i.e. revenue = customers; materials = costs; etc.

- Aside from obvious tactical decisions and actions, maintain perspective on your level of patience and perseverance

Memo #16
To: Dan
Re: Monitoring Cash Flow

MENTIONED I AM MORE OF A VISUAL LEARNER. One of my best experiences from an outside advisor dealt squarely with managing cash flow. Bill had just returned to Court Products with his new plan to revitalize the business. At that point, John had also put us on notice that he no longer would be acting as Court Products' bank. John did, however, have one of his advisors, a business consultant, come into our business to discuss some of our problems with selling product. This business consultant quickly studied our financial picture and then took us into the warehouse. He asked for some rope and then promptly cordoned off a rather large section of shelving. He then turned around to the still accessible racks, pointed at them, and said "do NOT buy any additional product that would not be able to fit in this open space." He further asked us to identify the "dead inventory," those products that were not moving through with any regularity. Essentially, he knew our investment in inventory and he projected what level of turnover, or sales, we had to achieve above and beyond our current customer orders to manage to at least a cash flow neutral operation. It was highly impactful, and in retrospect, a hugely simple—and visual—lesson in getting focused on what it might take to have your business succeed.

In fact, I returned to this lesson when I eventually put my own plan in front of John to re-launch Court Products. From that point on, watching that cash balance and the factors that impacted our cash flow became my principal focus. I projected our ability to order product based on when expenses were due and the expectation receivables would pay in 30 days. As we began to look at the cash availability in our projections, the discipline in inventory selection and purchasing became acute. There were often times during those early months when we might have an order inquiry, but we didn't have cash to buy the inventory so we had to delay the customer. There is no greater disappointment than having that sale on the hook and not having the means to satisfy your customer or offer a substitute. Think of the impact repeated instances of this inability to serve your customers will have on the business—it is a prescription for disaster. All the more reason it was critical we gained a quick understanding of what sold, at what frequency, at what margin, to what market—so that we could better understand what company we had to become in order to be successful—let alone just survive.

As noted, part of our transition to the new business plan I put forward was that we had to liquidate a significant level of racquetball club inventory. This liquidation experience helped me realize one of John's most important lessons to me. He would always talk about treating vendors just as important as you would your all-important customers. He would say "always pay vendors on time, because you never know when you may need to rely on them for a favor." Court Products had been in business about 12 years prior to my coming along—and that principled approach to treating vendors fairly paid off at this critical survival point. At prices that thankfully didn't kill us, we were able to work with a few vendors to help anonymously liquidate that inventory destined for a market we no longer targeted.

Map Your Operating Cash Cycle. Early in your company's life, charting the cycle of critical aspects of your operating cash flow can provide early alerts to potential problem areas in your business plan. Many of the accounting and bookkeeping software packages today have the ability to create helpful visual aides to monitor cash flow.

Depending on your business, certain factors will be of more interest to highlight than others. In Court Products' distribution business, a basic cash flow cycle of inventory plus receivables less payables provided a ready picture of our progress in managing the cash investment of working capital in the business. Breaking it down by product types, end market customers, etc. also provides insight into areas of potential focus. When we were able to map working capital more consistently, adding in the more routine expenses of payroll, office expenses, rent, etc. then provided a much-needed window into cash forecasting and planning where only intuition and hope had operated previously.

As a distribution business, we did not have significant plant or equipment expenses for which to budget. As the business stabilized, our spending on computers and office equipment, warehouse shelving and staging and even our building became much easier to plan. For those businesses that do have a more substantial manufacturing element, understanding the complete cash cycle and the ability to build reserves to accommodate larger one-off expenditures for new equipment is a prime area of focus for the small business owner.

Cash flow forecasting is also important in understanding the business' ability to seize on a growth opportunity. Some cash decisions for growth are necessitated. For example, if you are manufacturing a product and sales are outstripping capacity, you either have to find the ability to outsource the manufacturing (which has quality control considerations attached) or you must invest in additional capacity yourself. This may also require additional headcount to run the physical asset. In a service business, expanded capacity results from adding people. That new expense is largely fixed in the short run; thus, you must budget carefully. Understanding the timing of when and how much the sales growth is planned relative to the investment outlays provides a picture on how your cash balance may initially be squeezed during a period of capacity investment.

At Court Products, we tried to project in a "stair case" model how an increase of $X of sales can support an investment of $Y in costs (inventory carry, personnel, etc.). Just like in manufacturing, however, there is no guarantee the level of sales growth remains. In a distribution business, the nature of the expense growth is admittedly more variable than that of a manufacturing setting. That is, it may be easier to liquidate inventory and reduce staff versus sell off a big piece of equipment without taking a sizeable loss.

KEY TAKEAWAYS

- Charting the cycle of critical elements of your company's cash flow can help provide early alerts to operational problem areas

- Don't rely on intuition to measure cash flow, track tangible performance measures

- Without strong cash flow management, planning for large, one-off expenditures or growth opportunities is next to impossible

Memo #17
To: Dan
Re: Driving Sales, Managing Costs and the Income Statement

SALES MANAGEMENT. Understanding exactly who will ultimately benefit from your product or service and what path they will take to obtain it (recall Memo #8—Strategic Analysis) is the key to understanding how to organize a sales approach. Despite a national customer base, we don't have a dedicated "sales department" among just the six of us in the office. Rather, as a small business, we have had to develop a sales methodology. To do this, we try to understand the organizational approach of the networks we sell to and apply as efficient a coverage program as we can afford based on our expectations of the revenue opportunity. Importantly, we connect with our customers to educate them on not just our offering, but the service we can provide.

National not-for-profit clubs and public organizations with regional or local affiliates generally leave the buying power with the local operation. These local operations are subject to standards set by a national office in order to preserve, in a sense, a brand. Thus, in-person calling on the head office isn't going to effectively advance our sales efforts. Occasionally, there are national meetings and conventions where they invite vendors like us. This becomes a much more efficient way to establish the level of contact we need deeper into the actual buying entities.

Within the regional or local affiliates, it is also important to understand how they make their purchasing decisions. One of our customer organizations may have tens or hundreds of regional and local affiliates. Further, there are subsets of these affiliates that have different types of facilities which drive alternative offerings of classes and programs. This multiplier effect impacts the breadth and quantity of apparel and equipment orders. It is incumbent upon us to know the individuals on point for these classes and programs.

Our sales effort is coordinated around the annual catalogue (both online and paper). The catalogue targets various clubs and organizations and highlights product that fits their respective national standards. During the last 30 years covering my time at Court Products, the internet has, of course, profoundly impacted all businesses. We continue to believe landing a physical paper catalogue on the desk of a person with purchasing responsibility helps drive our top line. Think of even your own mailbox, particularly around the holidays. There is, however, no denying we have stepped up our online offering to notify our customers of new product opportunities that emerge in an almost continuous stream. In fact, the internet has likely helped product driven organizations fine tune their offering in a more realistic real-time sense.

When we relied solely on a paper catalogue, we may have marketed a product line that fell flat and then led us to a difficult sales year. While today the paper catalogue is still locked in upon distribution, our internet offering can more quickly react to, and compensate for, a weaker paper catalogue launch. The critical aspect is not to overwhelm your entire customer list with junk e-mail, rather we take more time to consider how to segment our market and offer targeted, viable and valuable product updates. You can't send your customers every new product as it comes along. You must view yourselves as the knowledgeable party, though always thinking from their perspective. Then, consider your own investment limitations and margin potential and initiate the appropriate interim sales strategies.

Getting the "word out" is one thing, but what ultimately drives sales, particularly in our business where product is generally readily available, is a service focus. If important to the customer, Court Products will sell that customer a quantity of one. If you have a volume driven business, maybe you wouldn't be able to do this all the time. If your customer knows you are prepared to be flexible when they need it, however, this goes a long way in building a lasting business relationship. The same goes with our vendor relationships. Their responsiveness goes hand in hand with our ability to offer great service.

We have a small office, so we all can essentially hear what is going on. We have established price parameters around our products and quantities so our team can confidently respond on the phone or web at any moment to our "best and final." It is the philosophy under which we buy, and it is the same under which we sell. Customers want to know they don't have to "take it up the line" in order to get the best price on offer. We also do not push a "flavor of the month" approach to sales. We listen to what our customers need and then go about sourcing it. Make no mistake, we do end up overstocked on some pieces of inventory, but that is what a SALE is all about.

In terms of driving sales growth, understanding how your customers use your product or service and how long it lasts is important in determining how much effort you need to direct toward your existing customers versus seeking out new customers and markets. If you have established your brand and image with a particular market, you don't need as much incremental sales effort and marketing cost to push more product. There may be limits to expanding your top line within your existing market. The local oil change service shop will not have much luck convincing their customers of the need for an oil change every 1,500 miles. Expanding to new markets then requires you to circle back to that cash flow forecasting exercise in order to determine how much you can invest to profitably grow.

Connecting with and educating your customer base is one thing, it is another to actually study their response. To do this effectively, we revert back to our financial strategy reviews. Importantly, high level, generic revenue headings may not be enough to help you determine the true course your business is on. You may need to break down your revenue analysis by product, by service, by customer class, by week, by day—whatever it takes to ensure your business is not straying off course toward potential financial problems. Coupled with a strong focus on costs (see below), you will have the key inputs you require to monitor your day-to-day financial progress.

Today, there are multiple options available for customer relationship management ("CRM") software packages to improve the analysis of customer information. They can record key contacts, track sales calls/visits, inquiries, order histories and even highlight when it would make sense to follow up with a client to remind them of their historical buying routines. While maybe not something you need immediately, as your business grows, it is a far better solution than Post-it notes on your computer screen.

Cost of Sales, Vendors and Production Management. The process of buying a car can be fraught with anxiety. It is routinely thought of as the second most expensive purchase you make in a household. You go to one dealer and attempt to settle in on a vehicle model, style, color, range of options, etc. Then you enter into the negotiation ritual around price. Today, since auto dealers effectively have the same product offering, or at least access to, you can play off one dealer's price to another. It is an accepted consumer buying ritual.

Running a small business, I discovered I just did not have the time in my days to play this game with the range of vendors we had. We must be competitive to earn our customers' business, so we will be equally demanding of our vendors. In cases where we have some particularly large orders, we will solicit multiple quotes. Competitive and interested vendors will come back to us and ask if they won the order. In the majority of cases, the losing bids for these jobs were those that were not price competitive (given our rather generalized product offering). Upon learning they lost based on a price criteria, I often would then hear "you should have told me, I could lower our bid." My standard reply was "if you get to lower yours, do I give the other guy a chance to lower theirs?" I would further add "if you want our business, then give us your best effort up front." Otherwise, the back and forth will never end. You settle with a bad reputation among your vendors and you have customers waiting for product while you dither to and fro among vendors. Thus, we employ "ethical bidding." Our vendors learn our approach during their first encounter and, frankly, most appreciate the candid exchange and set us on our preferred "best and final" response mode.

This negotiating sport is not unique to any particular type of business; it occurred during bids on projects in the pool business, as well. It is, however, important to keep your core vendors honest and competitive. Thus, a broader solicitation of bids for supplies or services is warranted on occasion.

You also may learn from your vendors of new products, services, processes or production methods to address customer needs you are trying to satisfy. Consider your vendors an important source of market knowledge to assist in delivering the best result for your own customers. A sign of a committed vendor relationship is when they financially assist you in bringing a new initiative to market. They have obviously analyzed the benefit for themselves, but it speaks to their confidence in your business. Depending on the way your customers are organized and operate, they may not be set up to have their own buyers looking out for changing technologies or enhanced service approaches. They are then relying on you. Some of our vendors have earned a product spot in our catalogue for bringing what we viewed as a value-added idea even if the price wasn't the "best available."

A factor to consider when choosing vendors is their ability to help you respond quickly to your customers. In order to earn this "favor," we have always felt we have to treat our vendors fairly. By that, I mean reasonable turnaround demands, ethical bidding, and on-time payments. Pricing may be the critical component for delivering on a large order if there is any hope to make a decent profit. Not all sales, however, are big ticket orders. By cultivating our vendor relationships, we have been able with their assistance to produce a single item run to put in front of a customer in the hopes of winning future business of a meaningful size.

Another caveat about knowing your vendors is whether you have a good handle on their own financial stability. The more your business relies on one key vendor to supply materials or service to your operation, you need to understand the impact on your own business were that vendor to fail and suddenly close its doors. You will need to quickly replace a potential key operational input in short order without disrupting your own customers. This can be difficult to monitor in the world of private small businesses; however, you do have the ability to talk to key vendors and gauge their view of business flow, monitor order fulfillment timeliness and quality as well as dispute settlements, or maybe even order a credit report. This is one more thing your business must monitor, but if you are going to make a single vendor a critical link in your supply chain, pay close attention.

Where your business is driven by maintaining some level of inventory, an area of consideration is to what degree you can purchase a broadly available basic input or stock item. And from whom. You must determine whether you are reliant on some vendor's private line or you can comfortably survive off an industry-wide comparable offering. For example, in our business, we could choose to buy from only one apparel manufacturer. If, however, we put out a catalogue focused on that manufacturer's line and they then eliminate the line, we are stuck.

One aspect that does require some discipline and control is to restrict the desire to solve one of your vendor's problems by buying overstock and sticking it all into your own warehouse. In retail and wholesale businesses, closeouts tease you with a price lure. If it is on closeout, it should be a yellow flag as to whether your customer base will find it any more appealing than the vendor's other markets. You must carefully evaluate these "can't miss" inventory deals to understand if you can truly fill your customers' underlying basic need vs. the cost to carry that closeout. The liquidation of a non-spoiling raw material like galvanized steel pipe could benefit a fence business, but you still need to balance how much cash to tie up in your inventory investment. It is important to understand what level of investment your business may need to tie up at any one time in raw materials, work-in-process and finished goods inventory. There are countless other supplies and materials your business will consume. Be mindful of your investment in indirect materials—those not added directly to your product or service. Also be mindful of careful accounting so you can accurately cost out your per unit products and services.

For more complex products or services, such as a manufactured part with twenty components of differing metal alloys, it is also critical to understand the sum total of all the material inputs in order to properly price the product upon sale. A service business that bids on a fixed price basis must understand the required people and hours it will take to finalize the project. Monitor these direct people costs over time. If a production problem has arisen, you may be selling under your costs. If, on the other hand, you have become more efficient, you might be able to become more competitive and take market share. Either way, this becomes your gross profit or, on a piece rate basis, your gross margin. Below, we'll talk about operating costs which, when combined with the costs of goods sold, represent your total product costs. If your business is dependent on competitive bidding and you do not have an appreciation of the total costs to manufacture, sell and deliver your product or service, you are likely headed for some volatile periods of profitability. Underpricing the product quickly shows up in losses and can spell the end of your business venture.

Operating Costs and Administrative Cost Management. A temptation during a period of economic stress is to look at cutting every possible variable cost line item. Businesses, however, must keep in mind the nature of their core value proposition. For Court Products, providing excellent customer service is what we are all about. During the late 2007 to 2009 Great Recession, we stayed essentially flat in sales and we did not cut our marketing budget at all. It was imperative that our customers knew that we were still there for them and could be counted on to deliver the same quality products and service we always had. Independent data tracking of our markets does not exist. Quite possibly, while we stayed front of mind with our customers, our competition may have cut back on their marketing efforts. Our vendors commented on our business activity, thus we may very well have taken a bigger share of the market during that difficult economic stretch.

When it comes to advertising your product or service to your customers, consider whether critical components are already advertised on their own. For example, the branded athletic apparel we customize is well known and advertised nationally. Similarly, the decking company re-staining a deck doesn't have to mount a full-scale campaign around the benefits of its stain choices. Other small businesses organized around boutique retail shops similarly benefit from the marketing provided by the manufacturers of the shop's array of inventory. If you don't have to be the one to spend to educate your customer on the latest evolution of product developments, use this to your best advantage. By riding the advertising coattails of brand-name manufacturers, the expense layout of a bit of marketing and advertising cost is transferred from your budget to that of a big-name supplier.

Outside of marketing to our customers, I am a miser. I do view every expense as coming out of my wallet. Very early on, I would walk through the warehouse and pick up paper clips that had fallen during the receiving and sales fulfillment process. I would dust off those "units of currency" and put them back in the jar for re-use. They were not going to fall prey to the broom and dustpan. During my days at K-Mart, I wouldn't have given it a second thought; I would have left them for the night clean-up crew. If you have a manufacturing or assembly plant, scrap materials should be carefully recycled, inventoried for alternative use or sold for scrap. In small business management, you never know at what point every penny may count.

In general, however, even considering our catalogue production and distribution costs, projecting our cash needs around non-personnel operating expenses is one of the easier areas to get right. That said, depending on your location and the nature of your business, electricity for air conditioning and humidity control and heat for the winter sometimes require a rainy-day fund to cover seasonal anomalies.

For companies with plant and equipment requiring maintenance, there are some "must do's." First, a small business isn't likely to have back up machinery, thus it is imperative to provide scheduled maintenance requirements for equipment. That is no guarantee of freedom from breakdown, and these emergency costs must also be factored in to what it takes to produce your product. Training the in-house team on basic repairs for the plant and equipment in a small business is essential to get back up and running as well as keeping a lid on repair costs.

One operational cost most businesses must deal with is office/warehouse space. Think of Apple's spectacular new Cupertino, California headquarters relative to the garage in which it began! Importantly, growing out of your physical space, while a cost to relocate, typically signifies profitable growth. Securing too much space with the hope of filling it one day can be an early drag on costs, add to the overall product or service's total costs and cause you to lose sales due to your uncompetitive pricing. Part of your strategic and financial analysis (Memos #8 and #9) should focus around realistically judging your physical space requirements. Don't succumb to the temptation to fill your plant or warehouse space with machinery or inventory just to utilize the space. The cost to carry it can have a significant negative impact on your operating efficiency and financial health.

When it comes to operating expenses in a small business, personnel is a critical area of focus. Manufacturers typically need to ensure they maintain a quality skilled staff to operate and maintain the substantial company investment in equipment. When I first joined Court Products, which of course coincided with Bill's extended leave notice, one of our first tasks was to reduce the 13-person headcount. We'll discuss more about managing human resources issues next (File #6—CEO of HR; Every Day!), but the impact of headcount to your cost equation in a small business is a never-ending area of focus. Too few and people get stressed, they could make mistakes and impact your product or service quality. Too many and the profitability will take an immediate hit as does morale when the decision to downsize follows.

A quick comment before proceeding with other personnel cost considerations. As noted earlier, if you operate something like a consulting business, you might look at some of your personnel costs as direct product costs. How much time commitment from the class instructor does it take to prepare and deliver a two-day training seminar on Microsoft Excel? This is important for direct costing of the service. That instructor's classroom time is not the same overhead or staff expense category as the time spent in the office creating and preparing one of the company's general course offerings. Adapt to categorizing your costs to best enable you to manage pricing and overall cost control.

When managing the operational staff expense line, you also must be very attuned to managing the skillsets of the people you do have.

Whether it is an effort to reduce staff in response to a revenue decline or increase to seize growth opportunities, taking the time to evaluate the scope and quantity of skills your team has and whether they are aligned to their most productive use is a must.

When we have found ourselves stretched as a result of growth opportunity, we first re-assess to evaluate re-distributing work and/or reorganizing certain jobs. When the pace quickens as a result of more work all around, the tendency in a small business is to just look at who is free at the moment and assign them the responsibility. Resisting this easy fix and carefully thinking through the job mix and responsibilities can enhance your team's work satisfaction as well as improve productivity and control over your expense growth. On the flip side, unfortunately, you may also discover as your business changes, that someone on the team is no longer up to the task or capable of developing the skillset the company requires. Replacing that individual should also include a process to re-assess the remaining team to determine the precise skills the company must acquire. Finally, don't overlook the possibility of plugging a need with part-time or temporary help. Effective usage of such surge capacity improves the core team's attitude about job security.

The financial implications to the company of adding another person can be calculated for any business. For example, a $2 million sales company with a pre-tax, pre-owner payout margin of 20% means there is $400 thousand of profit (as defined here). Even an entry-level jack-of-all-trades addition to the team could very easily cost you in excess of $50 thousand per year (all in with benefits). To achieve the same pre-tax, pre-owner payout margin of 20%, your revenue line must grow 12.5% to hit $2.25 million—and there is still the same $400 thousand of profit owing to the increased expenses. Will hiring that full time person readily grow your business to preserve your income? Know the numbers and weigh your confidence in the opportunity.

One-time Costs. There will be instances in every business' history where even a straightforward sale hits an unplanned or unintended snag. Just as we re-launched Court Products, we shipped an order to a west coast customer addressing all their requirements. We then received a call they could not use them—by recommendation of the local police! As it was, the color palette of this order aligned to a certain gang and having children and young adults wearing the shirts could be a risk. We were just getting going and this was a strong customer. We ate the cost with an eye to a future strong relationship.

Having solid knowledge of your current financial condition as well as the financial cost of a one-off event will provide you helpful—but not all—the key inputs to determine resolution. What are the impacts to you and your customer now, to your respective futures, to your mutual relationship? Maybe there exists an equitable sharing arrangement. Either way, if the immediate cash impact is survivable, evaluate the range of long-term impacts before simply assigning guilt and payment responsibility.

KEY TAKEAWAYS

- The internet has driven real-time fine tuning of product and service offerings; sales strategies must keep apace

- Knowing how your product or service is used and how long it lasts will influence your effort to focus on repeat sales relative to accessing new markets

- Use vendors as a very important source of industry knowledge; both their word and their actions

- Know your investment in inventory at each stage of production; slow moving inventory prevents opportunistic investment elsewhere

- Knowing your total costs—materials, labor and admin support—is the only way to properly price your product or service, especially for competitive bidding businesses

- Consider an enterprise software solution to manage customer relationship data as well as sales, inventory and cost analysis

Memo #18
To: Dan
Re: Asset Efficiency and the Balance Sheet

WORKING CAPITAL MANAGEMENT. Cash, cash, cash. Whether greenbacks or bitcoin, it still makes the world go 'round. An important puzzle to solve is how much cash do you keep in the business. For some businesses, the protection and control of currency and coin creates a separate and much needed area of focus. Retail establishments must have very highly scripted process controls in place to safeguard the handling, depositing and withdrawal of cash. Point of purchase cashier terminals and technology have helped build in some of these necessary requirements to quickly balance sold inventory to cash received. For business-to-business operations, managing cash is more about how much is in the bank to cover the spikes of cash uses when the inbound flow inevitably does not match up. When selecting a bank, ensure they have satisfactory technology for you to transact, monitor and gain access to your currency needs when you require your cash balance information or the physical asset.

The earlier discussed aspect of cash flow forecasting works hand in glove with the consideration of how much to maintain in the business. Depending on the nature of your business operation, you must evaluate the eventual repayment source and timing of big-ticket required expenditures. Thoughtful planning is required for major expenditures like new machinery, buying your own commercial real estate or even preparing for a seasonal inventory purchase. In many instances that source of repayment will be an anticipated trail of future income/cash flow. Thus, if you are debt averse, your business will need to build rainy-day funds to accommodate planned or unexpected big-ticket purchases. This may mean postponing owner distributions, as well.

One final comment on cash. Based on your company's form of incorporation (see Memo #32—Legal Advice), you may be able to leave cash in the business without worry of every withdrawal causing a tax event. Working with your attorney and accountant can help you manage liquidity in such a way that permits greater flexibility to manage both your business and personal needs.

Collecting receivables is hopefully a routine exercise—98+% of the time. Again, depending on the business, you may have certain challenges. In the cash retail business, this is of little concern. Though, as an individual consumer yourself, awareness with credit card fraud demonstrates there is always some level of risk. Selling product or service to consumers or businesses in higher risk categories may necessitate your business planning for a certain bad debt expense level. As such, you must remember to price this expected loss into your product as it represents a cost of doing business.

In the main, however, receivables collection is a fairly standard process completed by employees that are often processing tasks according to set rules—set by both the collector and the payor. If you have fulfilled your end of the contract, you owe yourself every economical effort to collect your due. The nature of your business may also dictate how your customers pay. In the not-for-profit and public sectors, the cash cycle tends to be longer. That said, Court Products is consistent in setting out expectations, diligent about communicating according to a formal late notice process, and willing to escalate where action or responses are stalled. Just as we established our commitment to pay vendors timely, our collections policy expects fair play on the other end of the spectrum. If worse comes to worst, there are bad debt collectors you can hire. Further, customer defaults and repeated late payment actions should prompt a review of your willingness to conduct future business.

As a distribution business, the discussions we have about monitoring our cash flow and watching our costs of goods sold clearly highlight inventory management as a prime area of focus. Inventory can kill a business two different ways. Overbuying too much inventory can choke the company with payables and heighten the chance your product could fall out of favor or become unusable before sales materialize. Conversely, under-buying inventory can lead to backorders and angry customers that stray to your competition to receive the service they deserve. The goal is the ability to manage to that level where you can comfortably exist between plastering the word "SALE" on a pile of slow moving product and having to over-service a valued client due to a slow order fill.

In manufacturing or assembly businesses, consideration for the amount of purchased inventory must also include the length of the production cycle. Such a business will require sufficient raw materials available to feed the production line. An amount will be tied up in work-in-process for the period of the production cycle and there will be more sitting in finished goods awaiting shipment. An investment in this total inventory is critical to meeting market demand and represents a permanent investment in your capital assets.

Managing Fixed Assets. Businesses requiring an array of machinery and equipment must be equally careful not to overinvest. Idle equipment does have a cost as it was capital expended which is now not available for other uses, including owner dividends. If internal capacity is running tight, have backup plans in place where you can run additional shifts or outsource production. If that is not feasible, gauging the stepwise investment required to support a given level of growth can be a constant challenge.

Financing commercial real estate is an offering of virtually every bank. Bankers love the physical nature of that collateral—despite the fact that some real estate cycles have broken many a bank. Even if you are able to run your business out of your basement off a laptop, the fact is you need some physical space to operate. Leasing and buying options are often plentiful; however, the nature of the business can limit choices. You can't obviously establish a metal scrapyard in the middle of a downtown. You also might second guess buying a retail franchise on a country road with sparse traffic. Choosing where to locate your business may be dictated by its nature. If you are selling local crafts in your small town, you should probably seek a shop on Main Street. On the other hand, for Court Products, we have a national customer base and thus had flexibility to locate to a building/warehouse close to my home and fitting the expense parameters of our business. Furthermore, our customers do not visit our base of operation, so we didn't need to have a bucolic office park view. If you do have visiting clients or customers, selecting an appropriately comfortable and aesthetically pleasing office is more important.

One consideration when choosing a location is the disruptive impact to your business of a move. If moving locations is a logistical nightmare and carries a fairly high cost, then securing a long-term lease or an outright purchase may be more appropriate—despite cheaper short term lease options. Lease terms, once exhausted, then inevitably raise the specter of rent increases. Court Products experienced this shortly after I took control. The owner from whom we leased sold the building and the new owner significantly raised the rent. Based on some of the above considerations, we found a much more spacious alternative where a new mortgage to own was cheaper than renting.

Valuing Business Assets. A word about balance sheet thinking in periods of stress. One approach to valuing a business is to assess the value of the underlying assets. Assets are meant to have some value, but don't fall in love with the values your accountant has assigned on your financial statements. If the unfortunate circumstance arises wherein you must sell assets to address a difficult business environment, or even worse winding up the company, it just always seems to be the case the assets are not worth as much to others as the cash and sweat you invested yourself. Nobody should capitulate and give away value, but timing (i.e. during a recession) dictates you have to be brutally honest with yourself about such values.

KEY TAKEAWAYS

- Managing cash can be both a control concern for the currency and coin, but also a budgeting issue to account for seasonal or big-ticket purchases

- An investment in inventory is a permanent investment of capital for a going concern; plan carefully for seasonal or one-off sales promotions

- Maintaining sufficient production capacity requires capital budgeting planning with ample foresight

- The physical premise needs of your business require careful consideration: purpose, space, location, growth potential—then you must evaluate whether to lease or buy

Memo #19
To: Dan
Re: Other Operational Challenges

QUALITY CONTROL. I cannot come up with a business where a product or service somehow can be delivered uniformly perfect time after time. That is, a business where there is no need for some element of quality assurance or quality control. Without getting too technical, some define quality assurance as the ability to monitor and fix the product or service while in the process of production or delivery. Quality control then is the process of looking at a completed production process, analyzing the collective result and making any necessary procedural changes to improve on the next "run." For our purposes here, I am referring to all of this as quality control. In either case, ensuring top quality for a small business is one of the most important operational processes you must have in place.

The very nature of a small business is one where the financial capital base is very modest, the product or service breadth is rather narrow and the target customer base may be limited. Repeated mistakes resulting in delivery of a poor-quality product or service can tear through your reputation quickly and destroy all hope of recovering to your original vision of a successful enterprise. It is also important that you, or the business as a whole, do not develop hubris and believe that your operation is perfect—every time, all the time.

Once Court Products was up and rolling after our re-positioning, we gained more confidence in the amount of product and the breadth of designs we would offer. When we believed we had produced a solid design offering that could be marketed to multiple regions of a national organization, we began to pre-order larger quantities in anticipation. This would allow us to achieve lower average unit costs, deliver quicker, cut down on back orders and keep complete orders flowing. One season we produced an initial batch of shirts and started selling the product. A few days in, we received one call—soon to be followed by too many others—that we had misspelled the word "Communities" as "Communties" on every single shirt in this large pre-order.

This was not only a miss out the door. We had the opportunity to catch this in our proof with our printers and we missed it there too. The cost went beyond just eating all the shirts by destroying the inventory, we also incurred the cost to pick up the shirts we had already shipped. What we could not measure was the impact to our image. We looked careless, sloppy and it was one of our most embarrassing lapses. As a result, we now do actual product samples for the items in our catalogue that we can "proof" before we do an inventory run. The art design programs even have spell check and we have a checkpoint to ensure that task is completed. Everyone in the office is now part of the catalogue reading and product review effort.

Documenting Formal Processes. A small business cannot become a robotics factory. There never seem to be enough hands for the many tasks required and completion of those tasks are constantly being re-prioritized. Additionally, you will likely find your teammates need to cross-train so they can fill in for sick or vacationing colleagues. To ensure consistency, we have created desktop procedures for many of our administrative tasks such as receivables and payables processing, check writing, deposit preparation, credit card processing, etc.

Looking at those tasks that require solid consistency, but may be subject to multiple hands should help you decide where a good set of desktop procedures might be useful. For example, to improve our customer service, we need to ensure our customer service representatives can respond as thoroughly as possible to the broad range of customer inquiries. As such, we created a grid to establish the authority to offer volume discounts, rebates, etc. For those that don't fit the procedure, it does make sense that Dan or I should be involved.

Businesses where cash and inventory control are important should also establish written procedures. It can also provide some protection when personnel evaluations are prepared by setting clear job expectations and performance standards. Your employee manual (Memo #27—Protecting Yourself) should refer to these job aides. For manufacturing and processing facilities, written procedures can also help facilitate safety precautions in addition to acting as valuable job aides. Should your business be based on creative content (i.e., design, consulting, etc.), the benefit for such documentation should clearly follow just the administrative aspects of the project.

In many respects, written procedures do help convey basic expectations and explain to teammates why a particular task is important. This latter element to our desktop procedures is an effort to avoid the exercise coming off as if I was saying "do this because I said so!"

KEY TAKEAWAYS

- Poor quality product or service will have a direct negative impact to your company's reputation— and profitability

- Quality and consistency for administrative tasks can be improved with documented process instructions

File #6

CEO of HR (Every Day!)

Memo #20
To: Dan
Re: Your Most Critical Role

BY THE TIME YOU FINISH REVIEWING THIS SECTION on managing the team dynamic, I think you will know this is one area in which I know I still have much to learn. I have definitely not mastered the human condition! What I have learned, is that you may have invented the best widget ever made, built the best office/warehouse for your business, created the most innovative and inviting website, but if you don't have the right people in the right positions to get the right work done—it will all be worthless! Your team must all work together to enable that well-oiled machine to produce the results you and your customers expect.

Lynn worked for two Dow 30 companies. Just think for a moment when you work for a company with over 200,000 employees how many are named Smith or Jones. Think also about how many departments, business lines or even teams within those units that have multiples of workers than I ever had in my entire company. The fact is, when you work day-in, day-out with but a handful of people in a small business, you frankly get to know them as closely as if they were your own family. You literally cross paths hundreds of times a day.

Big corporations have their chief personnel officers. I'd like to tell you that the first person you hire in your business should be your Vice President of HR, but . . . as the President, CEO, Managing Partner or whatever you wish to call yourself, no role in your company will be more critical than your being Head of Human Resources/Personnel. Your business may be focused around a specific product, service, patent, etc., but if you cannot find the right mix of people to form a cohesive small team, the distractions mount and the business will struggle.

One challenge the small family business faces is the inherent promotional ceiling for non-family members. We all want to find talented, highly motivated individuals with professional ambition and a passion to lead. As the owner of a family-owned business, you simply may not be in a position to offer such individuals the long-term opportunity they seek. Consequently, you may not always find the deepest pool of highly qualified applicants from which to choose. You can, however, stress the experience of working in your small business could provide a highly motivated and highly skilled employee a window to witness, and maybe experience, a more complete range of the necessary operating activities of a company.

There have been many twists and turns with my small business over the years—the initial gut-wrenching stretch to profitability, the pilferers, the resignations, the illnesses, the Great Recession (late 2007 to 2009), and bringing on board my son. Without question, the hardest task I ever have had to do was to let someone go from their job within our business' small family—and it has remained that way to this day.

KEY TAKEAWAYS

- Ensuring the right people are in the right positions to do the right work is fundamental to success

- Attracting highly talented, great leaders is complicated by the inherent career limitations within a family-owned business

Memo #21
To: Dan
Re: Hiring and Forming
the Right Team

PREPARE, THEN HIRE. Whether you are in need of building the human resource element of your business as your idea begins to take shape or you buy into an existing business (akin to my situation), you need to develop a method to inventory the skills your team has, the skills it requires and the skills it will out-source (Memo #5—Do You Have the Necessary Skills?). Once you have that exercise complete, you also should conduct a very honest personal assessment of the type of person with whom you can best trust, communicate and enjoy (Memo #4—Is Your Personality the Right Fit?). Don't overlook this last factor. You will likely spend more waking hours with your team than you will with your family—it can't be a drudge to get through the day. Otherwise, you will find your family sending you right back to the office because you are bringing a bad attitude home.

For the initial team, that skill inventory depends on how well you have evaluated your business' strategic needs (Memo #8—Strategic Analysis). There may be roles in your business requiring specific subject matter expertise (i.e. website coding for a web design firm) or a regulatory license (i.e. lawyer, architect, doctor, etc.). There is also likely to be a need for some teammates to be called on to address multiple roles and responsibilities. In my business, I could hire an accountant, but we wouldn't be able to provide them a full-time role. Thus, simply choosing highly specific subject matter experts must be balanced by the knowledge that versatility may also be valued.

I have a "friend of a friend" who owns a few McDonald's franchises. His #1 task on the time consumption chart is the need to continuously find new talent. Now, flipping burgers at an entry level may not equate to finding folks looking for a career role, but for the franchise owner, it can be a difficult and constant time requirement of the business. The fact is that franchise owners number a significant force within the small business community. The franchise owners are the career element of this type of small business and it just so happens one of their critical "raw materials" is part-time talent. Without it, the business will suffer. If you intend to pursue franchise ownership that requires a significant number of entry-level, minimum-wage employees, prepare to make hiring and training a constant and important element of your day.

An important first step in finding talent is to familiarize yourself with the labor laws of your state through your attorney. This may impact your hiring process and pace. Avoiding time consuming, resource draining and generally distracting mis-hires is critical.

One of the most important policies in my business is that each new employee begins as a 90-day probationary hire. You may need to check the employment laws of your state to determine your ability to use such an approach. This trial run affords the existing team a meaningful opportunity to evaluate the skills and adaptability of a new teammate. It simply doesn't matter how good a person is, if the fit and personality cannot gel with the boss and the team, you are otherwise introducing a toxic exposure to the business.

For any new hire, be it at start-up or along the way, it is important to determine as early as possible whether that person is "on side." In a small office, you can hear quite a bit if you task yourself with being observant without coming across as a snoop. Depending on the business, you may have to step outside your normal routine and be the one accompanying a new hire to sales calls or make more frequent visits to the manufacturing floor. In an office setting, you can hear who is grabbing the phones to help customers, who is pounding on the keyboard entering data—these observable behaviors of a potential new hire can tell you quite a bit even before a more formal debrief with the existing team. Once your business is operational, chances are you will develop a conditioned gut feel for how things work when they are working well. Of course, clock watchers are fairly easy to spot just as those that never volunteer for anything beyond assigned duties. Contrast those personalities with someone exhibiting appropriate inquisitiveness to learn how the entire business operation comes together.

Versatility. One of my most enlightening exercises as the owner is taking the opportunity to work at each of my company's critical roles. This can provide you with the insight necessary to determine the kind of person and the set of qualifications and skills you need to fill a vacancy. It is one thing to casually observe when going about your own routine, it is entirely another to spend a day in someone else's shoes. Another derivative benefit of this effort is that each time you are faced with a role vacancy for Job A, it is an opportune time to re-assess your current team and best align them to their own skills. You may then decide to hire a replacement not for Job A, but rather Job B.

Were you to buy into an existing business or, like me, find yourself taking over an existing business, you might have to re-assess the current team to ensure you have the skillsets to achieve your goals. What can be very difficult, however, is the anxiety which builds in any workplace where changes are afoot and uncertainty abounds. In this instance, moving forward quickly and decisively is important to avoid turning a team against you or leaving them the impression that employee relations will be tenuous under your leadership.

When I took over Court Products, I was fortunate to have worked with the existing team for nearly two years. Not that I had been focused on making major changes since I had joined, but I certainly had an opportunity to assess each person's strengths and weaknesses across the necessary skillsets we would require. As mentioned, we reduced staff from a peak of 13 to seven just prior to my re-make of the company. The seven was going to have to be reduced to three, at best, to see if my trial makeover effort could succeed. For those I targeted for staying on, I rather openly discussed the plans for the new company and what I envisioned their role to be. To ensure I didn't launch with a team that might then turn around two months later and tell me "this isn't what I want to do," I began by asking them what they enjoyed about their role so I could ensure a reasonable fit.

Getting down to just three people means you need very versatile players that are team oriented. Someone is routinely going to have to pitch in for someone else and we were effectively starting a new company. As such, my knowledge of the detailed business operational flow was mostly an educated guess. Literally, this team would have to be well-versed on handling customer service, order entry and fulfillment, invoicing and receivables collection just for starters on the customer side. While we had had a couple of people very skilled at certain aspects of the old company, I ended up going with two people I felt had the willingness and motivation to be versatile team players that are the "jacks of all trades."

Energy, Drive and Confidence. Despite having the opportunity to hire people I had been able to preview for nearly two years, like all businesses, I eventually encountered turnover and the need to keep hiring. If there is one hiring criteria that stands above the rest, I would have to say "energy." I will listen to any applicant with energy.

For small business, that need for personal energy derives in part because any one of our teammates must be ready to handle the full range of roles and responsibilities. As noted, if someone is on vacation or out ill, our work force could be down 20%. We need to keep it all moving. To do that, per Lynn's management mantra, we need people with the energy to "step up, don't look up." I can't be there to tell them what to do at every turn. Even for new hires, we don't have a lot of idle time to provide extensive training. If a new teammate can demonstrate new and better ways to complete our tasks and procedures, I am very willing to hear from these new voices. In a business with a vision of great customer service, that energy translates into an outgoing, engaging and upbeat phone contact for our customers. That energy level tells our customer they are speaking with someone knowledgeable, someone that can execute and someone that can solve a problem.

Friends and Family. Finally, here are a couple of considerations about hiring family and friends. I had one young man, James, that worked our warehouse for four years and he was one of my best employees ever. Never mind he had to use trains, buses and walking to get in every day. He became so proficient at the warehouse, he came up front to work the phones on his slow days, took the orders, entered them and then retreated to pack and ship. One day James told me he was moving to Colorado. Recalling my years in Wyoming, truth be told, I was jealous. I knew he had a brother and I felt I "owed him" so I asked if James thought his brother would want the job. To his credit, he wasn't sure he wanted to recommend his brother because he wasn't confident in the fit. I should have listened, but I wanted to help his brother out and hired him anyway. It didn't take long before I realized James was the one in the know. Thankfully, before we hit that difficult conversation with the brother, he came to me and told me he was going to move overseas! Good advice and insight can come from any person at any level in your company. Recognize the position of knowledge they have and weigh those inputs carefully.

On another occasion, the son of one of our neighbors was looking for work. I was careful to have the candid conversation with my neighbor laying out my concerns if things didn't work out well. It blew up in a week, but it was all on the young man. He was drifting and didn't know what he wanted to do, but he was able to tell me after one week that working at Court Products wasn't it! In some ways, I was disappointed we didn't have any time to help him on his career discovery, but you can't solve all the neighborhood's problems.

KEY TAKEAWAYS

- Consider you will spend more time with your teammates than your own family—choose wisely

- As owner, work a day in each role so you truly understand the requirements and skills

- Be open and honest with candidates about what you envision the required traits and skills must be for roles within the company

- Use caution and be upfront about expectations when hiring extended family and friends

Memo #22
To: Dan
Re: Interviewing New Hires

READ THE HELP WANTED ADS and you will soon realize the person you seek is in high demand. Like others, we seek flexible, energetic, highly-motivated teammates. We want people that can demonstrate the desire to learn our business so that they will be knowledgeable, confident and helpful to our customers.

You will also discover the hiring process is time consuming and costly. You should be able to screen out ill-fitting applicants based on their credentials relative to your company's present needs. Given other demands on your time, an employment agency might also be of help in the screening process (see Memo #38—Employment Services Agency). Alternatively, there are also software packages you can buy that facilitate the applicant screening and hiring process. Hiring is time consuming in and of itself, but the real investment you will make is in the training of a new hire. As such, you want to get it right as best you can. That said, you won't be able to foresee every change in life circumstance that prompts one of your team from notifying you one day that they are leaving. To improve our odds of getting to the right type of individual, we typically involve the majority of the team in the interview process to ensure multiple points of view and multiple perspectives to interpreting answers to similar questions.

Question with Purpose. Interviewing is largely a matter of personal style. What is important is to realize what your style is because it could bias you toward particular individuals. Bias does not just include those issues that leap to most people's minds like race, religion, sex, etc. Negative biases (i.e. I readily reject a candidate asking about vacation policy during a first interview) can blind you to the exceptional qualities of a person (i.e. I love someone with a high-energy level). Likewise, overly positive biases could blind you to the faults of someone else. Be wary, this bias blindness can run in both directions. If you are starting a business that is going to require a high degree of sales time and effort and you are more of an introvert, maybe you shouldn't surround yourself with people just like you. Your company could struggle without someone that is comfortable getting out front as the public face.

When completing your own personal assessment of your personality traits and business skills, this is an excellent time to create a preliminary inventory of the additional skills your company is going to require. Importantly, what complementary skill are required? Take that preliminary inventory and keep that at hand as you evaluate your business' vision and strategy. Create a set of open-ended interview questions that will enable you to explore these desired traits and skills. You will need people of like-minded character and sufficient skill to execute on your vision and strategy.

I wouldn't consider myself the most difficult interview, but I know I also project a difficult to read set of reactions. As noted, when interviewing someone to join your small business, you want to assess the applicant's experience relative to the skillsets required to meet the demands of the posted role. In addition, I do ask people what their dream job is and how it engages them. An easy follow on here is to probe their previous roles and discuss what they liked and disliked about those jobs and the work environment. These questions begin to provide insight into a person's versatility as well as their willingness to be flexible. Both are important attributes for most small business teammates. I also ask them what they see themselves doing three to five years down the line. I am impressed by individuals with ambition, but frankly, in the small business arena, sometimes we are better served by those dedicated individuals looking for the right work/life balance and the willingness to be trained as a member of a stable team.

In our hiring process, one avenue of inquiry from a potential new hire that immediately raises the yellow caution flag to me is if someone asks "what is my job description?" This raises the distinct possibility that this person has perhaps worked in larger companies where roles are narrowed to increase efficiency. Some people, however, feel a need to be told exactly what to do and, once told, may well use that as a defense not to have to go "above and beyond" for the sake of the team and the business.

One other important source of interview topics I use is our employee manual. For example, we have performance categories for planning and organization, communication, etc. As discussed in Memo #27 (Protecting Yourself), we created the manual for multiple purposes, including setting performance expectations for ongoing appraisals. If that is the standard to which I expect to hold my teammates, then it should represent a decent starting point with which to evaluate prospective new candidates.

During difficult general economic times and depending upon your own ability and willingness to risk a short-term hire, there is potential for hiring a vastly overqualified person. In instances like this, plan to get the most out of this hire and think about having that individual address a specific project that you otherwise might have to contract out. Be transparent in your objective.

Team Decision? Involving the current team in the hiring process is a must. That said, you have to understand and appreciate the perspectives your teammates will bring to the notion of this new hire. Open communication with the team about what the person would be expected to do and how it would impact existing roles and responsibilities is the best way to get the team on side. We actually had one person that was with us for 17 years and was one of the two folks that helped re-launch the company. This person was a great recruiting asset for us as we could point to the potential for a stable, longer term job opportunity. At the same time, you have to remind your "recruiting" team that you remain the boss for each teammate, even new ones. If re-calibrating roles and responsibilities upon the addition of a new teammate is one of our company's core strategies, then routinely pushing the less desirable tasks toward the new hire is not exactly how it should work.

During a candidate's day of interviews or maybe on a second-round interview, you and the team should be talking amongst each other. If you have a candidate that is standing head and shoulders above the rest, instruct the team to go into "sales mode." Keep in mind that people coming into interview are also looking to join an engaging team within an exciting company. They are interviewing you, too! Let your pride and enthusiasm show when you have a positive reaction to a candidate. It may increase your chances of success.

Once we have made a decision to make an offer, in my experience, the issues driving most candidates' acceptance have usually come down to money and job flexibility. The latter includes not only total weekly hours, but also scheduling and vacation time. My desire to accommodate each of those factors is dependent on how well I think the candidate can step in and be productive.

- Beware of your own biases when interviewing; your team needs a diverse set of traits, talents and skills

- Ensure your interview questions help reveal that the candidate possesses the traits and skills required for the role as set out in your job description or employee manual

- To gain wider perspective, involve your current team in the process; it can provide an indication of "fit"

- Hiring can be costly and time-consuming; consider streamlining by networking or using an employment agency or software package

Memo #23
To: Dan
Re: Communications

SMALL BUSINESS OR LARGE, employees want to know what is going on with and within the company. Of course, the complexity of the company and any particular individual's standing may govern how much information should be shared. In a small business, it is hard to hide that much from anyone.

Meetings. We try to hold to a weekly meeting routine where we discuss performance as a team concept rather than singling out any individual. If we are experiencing a common error being made somewhere in the business, this is a great opportunity to empower a team and task them with finding ways to correct or avoid future occurrences. Similarly, maybe one area of the business is experiencing a backlog of work owing to our process. In this case, gathering the inputs of those on the front line is the only way to really get to the crux of the issue. If a change in approach is necessary, we then have the team's input as the driver of that change. We all know it is easier to accept change if we are part of the effort creating a better solution. I consider these sessions a win-win. The team gains empowerment and readily moves us forward and I am not branded a know-it-all possibly forcing something worse into action.

Regarding meetings, there is a significant difference between small businesses and large businesses. In a small business, the team needs to "meet to live." That is, they must quickly resolve an issue to fight another day. Dilbert cartoon-creator Scott Adams popularized the notion that large company employees "live to meet" as a means of establishing self-importance. Just ask a "large corporate" friend if they have been to any meetings with a dozen or more attendees where only three or four actually converse. Small businesses simply cannot afford to waste time with purposeless meetings when the livelihood of the business is at stake.

Along similar lines, while we do not have a formal "suggestion box," I have always stressed my door is always open. I certainly do not have all the answers, particularly for how best to carry out some of our specific tasks and procedures. I very much encourage suggestions on operational aspects like these. I have mentioned how I routinely step into each role on occasion to ensure I have a feel for what is happening and how we are responding. Nevertheless, even with this practice, keeping a pulse on everything happening every day is difficult at best. When it comes to your front-line team, assuming you are confident in those you have hired, you will have to develop an appreciation that they will help develop and perfect the best approaches to executing the range of tasks and responsibilities. Depending on the type of business and industry in which you operate, however, your personal involvement and careful appraisal of the safety and control implications arising from employee suggestions may be required. If you do not or cannot trust your team's input and judgment, it may be a sign you have the wrong people in the wrong places.

Monitor your Style. There are two other forms of communication about which any business owner should be aware. First is the notion of informal communication. As the owner, you should be careful not to overtly or inadvertently create a "teacher's pet." Take stock of your office conversations, think about who you engage at the coffee station or during lunch. Is it balanced? While unintentional, it may create some angst and jealousy among the team if you are disproportionately engaging with one or two teammates at the expense of the others.

There will always be one person that is willing to get into the details of yesterday's ballgame or last night's episode of Masterpiece Theater, just don't always fall down that rabbit hole with the same person.

The second is equally disruptive. It is the message communicated when an owner decides not to decide. Postponing, or flat out avoiding, making decisions does have ramifications across your business and can be a demoralizing influence among the team. There may be rationale behind your motivation not to decide—financial issues or maybe manufacturing or talent limitations. Within a small business, however, there are few secrets and you must realize non-decisions will frustrate your team. At a minimum, let the team know when to expect resolution. Similarly, be mindful of overtly pointing out when—and why—you are making an about-face relative to a previous decision. Nothing could be worse than the team losing confidence in your consistency and decision making.

KEY TAKEAWAYS

- Your teammates will talk to each other; get out in front of important topics with formal communication routines

- If done properly, communication becomes a two-way street and improves the overall business

- Be conscious of your informal communication habits; imbalance could cause team resentments

- Remember, choosing not to decide is a decision; at least communicate when you expect to resolve the question

Memo #24
To: Dan
Re: Formal Employee Reviews/Appraisals

FORMAL WRITTEN REVIEWS SHOULD BE CONDUCTED at least once per year. If you have identified performance issues, increasing the frequency to quarterly or semi-annually may be appropriate for a couple of reasons. First, you are hopefully remediating a productivity problem within the company. Second, if you wait too long and only relay concerns at an annual review, you could be setting yourself up for a prolonged disgruntled relationship that can infect other parts of your business and likely the rest of the team. Interim reviews such as these should also be well documented, clearly state the reasons for underperformance, what it will take to improve to a satisfactory level and when such a level should be achieved. Then, follow up and communicate as agreed.

We do provide our team with an appropriate notice prior to conducting reviews so they are also able to prepare and raise questions. Our review template is included in the employee manual so the team knows the criteria under which they will be evaluated. To address underperformance, an interim review may well be unannounced, though we certainly would allow the teammate time for some reflection and response. On the plus side, one of the nicest things about being a business owner is having an unannounced positive review that may very well end with news of a raise—a great feeling for both parties!

KEY TAKEAWAYS

- Your teammates deserve honest, thoughtful written reviews at least annually

- Underperforming teammates should be reviewed with greater frequency using a documented summary of issues and expectations

Memo #25
To: Dan
Re: Be a Good Coach/Mentor

ONE DAY WE HELD A BIRTHDAY CELEBRATION for one of the ladies on the team. At the time, we had this 17-year old boy that was working the warehouse for us. Well, we sang *Happy Birthday to You* and this kid very confidently asks "So, how old are you?" The guest of honor calmly replied "58." No sooner, the kid blurts out "Oh, I'd have guessed a lot older!" At this point, everyone is examining their shoe tops and making various attempts to re-direct conversation. In the end, however, an incident like this is a great teaching moment. Not right on the spot, of course, as you don't compound one error with another. Finding a quiet moment later with the young man to coach him in social graces can help in so many different ways—regardless, you owe it to whomever comes in the door. Think of it as paying it forward.

I made a car loan to a very dependable employee and did so partly because it was another great opportunity to coach. Sitting down with this young man and talking through the impact the dealer's very high 24% interest rate would have on the total amount of cash he would end up paying for his car was a valuable financial planning lesson for this young person. He was committed to dependably getting to work and bought a car to do so. We found a way to make it work for both of us and learn something along the way.

There are also instances where you can help educate your team on certain matters, but where you also must draw a line and not "decide" such matters. As a for instance, I have often been asked "how many dependents should I claim on my W-2?" I try to spell out the options and their impact. Too many will provide for a more sizeable paycheck now, but may require a tax payment come April 15. Too few and you have a smaller paycheck and perhaps a forced savings plan until the next April 15th. Try to think through the employee's issue and determine if it were to come out negatively for that individual, could you incur repercussions. You just don't want to plant the seeds of a growing set of other potential problems.

KEY TAKEAWAYS

- Small business teammates won't have many options to find mentors, be prepared to play the role

- Good coaching pays dividends later; even if the teammate doesn't stay, think of it as paying it forward

- Before an employee consultation, review potential negative outcomes; then determine if you can live with negative repercussions

I **N A SMALL OFFICE, YOU REALLY CAN'T AVOID** getting to know people on a personal level. Without intending to offend, here is my story of how personal it can become. If anything, this openly highlights my own challenge to maintain decorum. One woman on our team requested some time off weeks in advance. When the day prior approached, she thoughtfully reminded me she had scheduled the following day off. Not missing a beat, she also added that she didn't want me to be shocked upon her return and proceeded to inform me she was having breast augmentation surgery. Now, sharing that type of news pretty much pulls you into the family because I wasn't really on a need to know basis. I'm sure my face was brick red and all I was thinking was when she returns, what do I say, can I maintain eye contact . . . I was definitely at a loss. You will learn all about your teammates' families, spouses, kids, health and everything else you may not even know about your best friend—it can be fun, it can be taxing, but it is up to the boss to set the standard at being supportive and good natured. The best trait any boss can demonstrate is to show your employees you care.

Another delicate personal item is the assumption the team will hold that you, as boss, make the big bucks. They may very well come to you and ask if the company can make them a temporary loan. In my case, I have made small loans to help supply baby diapers to mid-size loans to pull a tooth. The latter problem was attributed to how hard the person was pressing the phone against their jaw while talking on the phone. The biggest was to that very dependable young employee that had his car repossessed by a "predatory" lender that stood to earn in interest more than three times the price of the car. Your greatest concern here is to maintain discretion, support a viable need, not venture beyond what you or the company should rightfully view as appropriate and document the agreement carefully.

Small business settings are not immune from petty office politics or playground bullying. Intellectually, it is interesting to consider how some people in a small office, where advancement in a family business is often limited, could become so rude to another teammate. Further, the ability to execute one's roles and responsibilities very likely hinges on the work and contributions of others in the office. With our vision of executing great customer service, we cannot afford interoffice petty arguments getting in the way. Disagreement between people is a certainty; as the leader, it is your job to step in and referee before such behavior negatively impacts the business. Candid conversation with the aggressor should highlight that life will get pretty hard on everyone if such behavior continues. The interconnectedness of a small business team does not allow for any teammate(s) to single out one individual with bullying. Your personal effort of privately meeting to hammer out disagreements should demonstrate to your team that being known as an agitator in your office is not the title to which one should aspire.

KEY TAKEAWAYS

- Knowing so much about each other has its positives and negatives; do show honest interest and demonstrate caring

- Supporting teammates beyond just a job requires discretion and discipline; know your limits

- Be prepared to shut down any inter-office bullying before it becomes a problem

Memo #27
To: Dan
Re: Protecting Yourself

IN 2004, I JOINED AN ORGANIZATION called TAB, The Alternative Board (more on this concept discussed in Memo #36—Board of Advisors/ Mentors). One issue that became clear to me during our discussions was the need to create an employee manual. Frankly, we had no such collection of employment policies. The guidance was that an employee manual would not only help consolidate and present the company's employment rules and offerings, it might very well serve to protect the company in the event of a disenfranchised employee. To that point, we were not immune.

For the manual, the lead chair of TAB provided me some documents and resources on where to start and some of my member cohorts provided me copies of their policies. I was then able to sort through various approaches but also select what was relevant to our own type of business. I also reached out to some friends in the small business community and then finalized it with a review by our attorney and obtaining signed copies of each employee attesting to their reading and understanding of the policy.

During the years without such a policy manual, we had fortunately not experienced any problems. About 5 years later, I had to dismiss an employee for a one-strike disciplinary issue spelled out in the policy.

That person, in turn, filed for unemployment. For a small company in my state, this one filing could increase my employer tax rate nearly 10 times the current rate. I filed a protest against the former employee's claim including a copy of the policy and the signed employee page. Fellow small business colleagues as well as several vendor associates told me I was wasting my time. In the end, however, our new manual actually helped us win the unemployment claim and maintain our lower unemployment tax rate—something countless outsiders told me would never happen.

Despite the family-like nature of the culture you develop within your company, you just never know when or why an employee might claim some unjust treatment which could lead to a lawsuit. As your company develops into a close-knit group, an employee manual does provide you a formal mode of backstopped support should you suddenly be faced with what can be a gut-wrenching dispute. Employment laws do evolve over time (usually to the favor of the employee), so it is worth re-visiting the content of your policy and refreshing employee attestations every couple of years.

Another avenue to utilize in protecting yourself are employment agencies (Memo #38—Employment Service Agencies). They are not just a feeder for potential new hires. Take the opportunity to tap their expertise on acceptable and legal hiring and/or firing questions and concerns. They can also be a good source for interview outlines and questions as these too have legal limitations. An employment agency we use has also provided input on our employee manual.

KEY TAKEAWAYS

- Create an employee manual to establish a code of conduct and obtain your team's signed statements of review and understanding

- Know the law on hiring and firing practices, including acceptable interview questions

Memo #28
To: Dan
Re: Downsizing and Firing

FOR ME, THE WORST ASPECT of being a small business owner is the responsibility of having to terminate an employee whether driven by business conditions, performance or cause. The latter may be highly justified, however, somehow one of the family strayed and it shakes your confidence in your ability to spot quality talent to join the team. As a young entrepreneur, you may be half the age of a working single parent you have to let go. I wish there was some sage advice to offer, but there is not. What it should do is build your compassion as you face other tough employee decisions over the years.

In my experience, when I had an employee that was not performing at the level necessary to justify their compensation, I felt I first owed that employee a duty to communicate and work on a corrective plan. The timing may or may not work in parallel with your annual review process. That plan should be documented as specifically as possible with set dates to measure progress. If the employee did not improve their contribution to the agreed level, I never found that our termination discussion came as a surprise. Using such an approach doesn't make it any easier during the termination discussion, but at least you can feel you have been transparent and fair.

When driven by business conditions, that always was a difficult conversation. Here you have a person that is, by all accounts, performing their role in a satisfactory manner, but the business just can't afford to support a staff beyond a certain number. As noted previously, if you build the right team, they become like a family and thus it becomes a very difficult decision and action. In these cases, I always did offer whatever support I could to provide a recommendation should the employee need one. Some might counsel against recommendations and have you only stick to discussing dates and compensation, but for someone that did their best for us, it's the least I could do to do the best for them.

Be Clear and Partner Up. For any job termination discussion, be clear, be concise and aim to keep the meeting short. Running on about what might have been may only provide the terminated employee with grounds for a later claim or lawsuit.

Further, whether business conditions, cause or performance, my experience in terminating employees has led me to require at least one other person being present so as to ensure clarity of message. This was highlighted on one occasion when the business was experiencing significant challenges prior to my re-launch. Two of our most senior employees scheduled a termination meeting for a Friday afternoon with a very nice person that was part of the team. That afternoon, one of those senior employees got stuck in an external meeting and the other, with his heart of gold, decided to proceed ahead alone. By all accounts, the discussion progressed amicably and the terminated employee finished up the day that Friday. The problem resulted on the following Monday morning when this same person promptly showed up for work! There just has to be another witness, an additional set of ears—and ideally a note taker—to ensure the script has been fairly followed and the message has been delivered accurately.

Be Professional. One of my worst experiences and regrets while at Court Products has to do with a downsizing event. John was the original capital behind Court Products and a woman named Sunny was his employee #1. The same Sunny that yelled encouragement out the door to me when I first joined (recall Memo # 10). The regret dates back to when Bill returned to attempt his revitalization plan. Bill must have been feeling the plan was not going well and our employee costs were out of line. Since John had communicated to Bill that I would eventually have the opportunity to take over, I was off the chopping block. My regret here was that I became Bill's operative. Given the ongoing financial stress, my role became delivering Bill's hard messages and reassigning duties that clearly came with the intonation that you were either favored or not. Bill directed too much of his angst toward Sunny. As the treatment became less professional and unbalanced, one day Sunny left for lunch, left her keys on her desk and never returned.

Sunny did not deserve that treatment, she was not a problem employee. I should have been able to stand up and push back, but I always felt these three had their own communication loop and that held me back from speaking my own mind. Sunny should have been told exactly what the business plan was and how she was intended to fit. At a minimum, she should have been offered the opportunity to accept a lower compensation package. Bill should have leveled with her, she had earned that over the years.

What does a young entrepreneur do with that experience. Unfortunately, I cannot reverse it, I cannot fix it, I cannot make it go away. I cannot change the hurt Sunny must have felt—and probably still feels. We all try to learn the best pathways to success, but we also should learn how not to fail at something so basic a second time. I vowed this to be a painful lesson I would carry with me every time I sat down with my teammates to talk about their performance.

KEY TAKEAWAYS

- Documenting underperformance or code of conduct violations is a must; stick to the facts

- In any termination conversation, have an additional company witness join to ensure clarity of message

- In a downsizing, be professional and be transparent; provide post-separation recommendations where possible

- And for the younger, less experienced entrepreneur, reach out to your network if you are unsure how to handle a given situation; explore the judgment, values and intuition of your collective network

- Ensure open communication and understanding exists when delegating sensitive personnel tasks to your team

NO MATTER THE BOND YOU FEEL YOU DEVELOP across your team and no matter the diligence adhered to when hiring new teammates, you will undoubtedly face a situation where some form of theft rears its ugly head. Most people might think of theft focused around cash, physical materials or merchandise or office supplies, but don't discount the impact of the theft of time or company trade secrets. Unfortunately, a small business is not immune to any of these.

Physical Items. Also raised in Memo #18 (Asset Efficiency and the Balance Sheet), cash may be a physical asset for which you must establish substantial controls. Any retail establishment must be prepared to deal with the physical flow of currency and coin. Registers must be consistently monitored and periodically cleared of excess. Customer sales and the working cash to stock registers and tills must be protected with an appropriate on premise safe. Bank deposit arrangements should become an important part of your banking relationship.

Within any company, however, cash also likely resides in each employee's wallet or purse. Throughout the course of the year, I used to periodically stash a few bills inside a green nylon wallet inside my briefcase that carried a few papers or trade magazines to and from the office.

I used this personal slush fund to amass a few bucks for spending on vacations, holidays or even buying gift cards to pass out for a job well done at the office. It went missing one day and it was one of those things where I looked virtually everywhere three or four times—but nothing. I was ticked off at myself for being so irresponsible!

After a year of moping about it, my wife bought me a new slush fund wallet as a Christmas gift (irony, huh!) and I slowly began to work up the nerve to begin my savings plan all over. At the office one day, I went to grab a gift card and, while the new wallet was exactly where I thought, it was cleaned out. I first yelled at myself for not remembering where I had spent it, but it began to dawn on me we may have a problem at the office. Against all my principles and wanting to have the trust in my team, I had a small camera installed in my office. Sure enough, an employee made repeated attempts to rummage my office, my briefcase and my slush fund wallet. I was personally devastated over several aspects, the only solace I took was that it was happening to me and not to a fellow employee. The theft was dealt with immediately by firing the employee. Your teammates deserve a trusting environment and when such a breach occurs, it must be dealt with immediately and decisively.

For businesses selling some form of merchandise, theft is something that somewhat comes with the territory. Your merchandise may not be like that at Court Products where we provide everyday apparel. Rather, you may have any manner of goods or even the raw materials to manufacture those goods that can be sold for some value on the street. I have had some very trustworthy warehouse assistants over time, but a few have found the temptation to pocket a shirt, jacket or shorts just too much. Companies with inventory always experience some shortage or shrinkage, sometimes due to erroneous shipments either inbound or outbound, but theft is a reality.

It is worthwhile to evaluate your inventory and think through the non-traditional avenues it may travel out the door or loading dock and periodically conduct some control watch or inspection. Of course, going so far as confronting a teammate for a search of a bag would need to come with pretty damning evidence. One of our shipping teammates would stuff apparel into trash bags and place them in the dumpster where he then picked the stolen items up as he quietly exited for the day. Yet another shipped goods out via UPS to a friend, had them sell the goods and then they would split the cash. I uncovered this scheme when UPS returned a boxed shipment. In the box, along with our merchandise, was a letter (that I still have) explaining the whole theft ring to his friend. Fortunately for me, the brains of the outfit used the wrong zip code on the returned package!

Intangible Items. The notion of the theft of time is likely something more noticed by fellow employees. That is the person that consistently seems to arrive about 15 minutes late or often has that end-of-day errand that requires an early departure. Think about it, 10 minutes a day is 50 minutes a week or about 43 hours a year—that person just milked you for another week of paid vacation. The greater cost to your business, however, is the impact this time thief has on other employees. As we all know, our personal lives require doctor visits for kids and plumbers' visits to fix faucets. Quite often those must be handled during typical work hours. We try to create an environment that works for all by having teammates properly request time to address such needs and then make up that time on another day. The high incident user, however, needs to be counseled early so it does not get out of hand and spoil it for everyone else.

Theft of trade secrets, particularly for a business built around a single innovation or intellectual process, can seriously damage your business, even drive it to ruin. Your employee manual should cover all types of theft, and theft of trade secrets should be clearly spelled out. When we re-launched the new Court Products, I came in early to find someone running off our customer lists, another critical asset of many companies. Still early in my career, I was not aware the damage that could result. It became evident he used those lists as he started a company that competed with us in certain aspects.

Theft is a demoralizing reality for a small business owner due to the tight relationships formed with the entire team. You will want to trust all your team implicitly; however, reality requires you to keep a watchful eye for the protection of your business and your fellow employees. When the proof is there, you will know what to do and you must just resolve the problem decisively.

KEY TAKEAWAYS

- It is your responsibility to maintain a trusting work environment, deal with problems quickly

- Get ahead of potential problems, think like a thief and figure out how your business could be exposed

- Employees stealing "time" can negatively impact the morale of the rest of the team

- Ensure theft, and its ramifications, are covered in your employee manual

File #7

Chief Administrative Officer

Memo #30
To: Dan
Re: Jack-of-All-Trades

THERE IS A POPULAR SAYING that somewhat describes the inherent nature of what a small business owner must become. It is a "Jack of all trades." On its face, it can be quite a compliment of one's diverse set of strengths. That said, sometimes you may hear the additional phrase "and master of none" added to the end. I would have to say that would be overly generalizing the small businessperson. It is true any owner cannot master every single aspect of running their business; however, you are the driving force of the idea behind getting it started, so you certainly mastered the critical one.

There may be, however, aspects of your business where you may not be best suited to build operational expertise in-house. Not because you can't, but rather maybe it is not the best use of your team's time and effort when you consider the myriad of actions and interplay necessary to deliver the actual product or service to your customer. Given the cost to achieve proficiency in certain professional specialties in something such as the law, a small business would not achieve the economies of scale to achieve a satisfactory return for hiring an on-staff lawyer. In general, the following memos discuss some of the administrative aspects associated with running a small business.

These are necessary disciplines and a few are essential proficiencies to be addressed by outside licensed professionals.

It could be a real bonus to you to be able to find a firm that bundles some services like legal, accounting and estate planning. Presuming one hand would know what the other is doing, the one-stop shopping approach enables the firm to get to know you and your business. You will spend less time educating and re-educating outside experts and hopefully more time having meaningful, coordinated dialogue. As will be discussed, many issues arising under the legal, accounting and estate planning headings have overlapping considerations. Such coordination may also save a bit on the cost in lieu of receiving three bills with minimum service charges or retainer requirements.

KEY TAKEAWAYS

- You cannot be expected to master every role within the context of your business

- Certain business proficiencies require licensed professionals; if not core, contract out

Memo #31
To: Dan
Re: Bookkeeping and Accounting

THERE IS A DIFFERENCE between bookkeeping and accounting. Think of the former as the data input for the latter. In other words, bookkeeping is the act of recording your company's range of daily financial transactions including sales invoices and receipts, bank deposits and withdrawals, purchase orders and payments and all manner of other expense and wage payments. Accounting, then, is the process of taking all this transactional bookkeeping data and aggregating it per accounting rules into the form of reporting used for managing your business, reporting regulatory requirements, and paying taxes. There are some excellent small business accounting software programs in the market today (such as QuickBooks) that facilitate the bookkeeping and accounting of a small business. Do take time, however, and compare features to the requirements of your type of business.

There are a few points worth stressing when it comes to bookkeeping and accounting. First, tracking the movement of cash and credit through the company must be completed accurately in order to ensure usable management information, lawful regulatory compliance and avoidance of theft. Hence, effective controls are necessary. Second, you can absolutely fall in love with your company's ability to deliver a certain product or service, however, if you cannot do so profitably, you may find your ability to survive severely challenged. Financial information allows you to keep a finger on the pulse of directional changes in profitability or cash and expense controls at detailed levels of your business operations. Finally, this information is more effective the timelier it is delivered. As previously noted, looking at this critical management information on a set schedule should be one platform of your business strategy.

When initiating a new business, be sure to begin tracking your expenditures very early. You are likely to experience many start-up expenses that keep tapping your wallet even as you begin the process of discovery. For tax purposes, many of these expenses may be deductible—if you keep track of them! As small as Court Products was when we reconstituted, I assigned the bookkeeping responsibilities to a person that had earned my trust and had displayed a relative comfort with numbers. Trust is hugely critical the more your business requires physical cash handling. Our business is more reliant on credit with payment through credit cards and checks. Further, as we were essentially re-starting a company without a fully confident view of near-term profitability, I wanted someone that could objectively handle the bookkeeping without spreading concern—overtly or inadvertently—about whether we were making suitable progress toward sustainability.

The person or persons entrusted with the bookkeeping responsibilities will more than likely gain a reasonable view of how well the company is performing. Even were you to break responsibilities up into incoming vs outgoing transactions, the pulse of business activity becomes readily apparent. As these teammates gain this greater appreciation for the business' activity, you may find they also develop a better feel for the business and what initiatives drive success. Eventually, these trusted teammates may be able to use this insight to develop as better internal advisors to you.

Instituting Financial Controls. Regardless of how you break up the responsibilities, you should institute some level of financial controls. It is important to let your team know from the early going that controls are straightforward good business practice and are meant for everyone's protection to help build team trust. It is not meant to be an insulting in-your-face challenge. In our case, I would take the bookkeeping inputs and complete the entire month end balancing and bank reconciliation. In the case of financial controls, obviously the quicker you can stop either a theft-based problem or even a data management problem, the better off you will be. Poor bookkeeping can lead to business and operational miscues that could exacerbate what may not have been a problem in the first place.

Your business may have operations that, when paired up with a book-keeping entry, could give rise to potential financial losses due to fraud or theft. For example, we do not permit the same person crediting accounts to also process the return of the physical items. We want an objective paper trail that the value of what was returned is equal to the value of the credit. Think of it as a "Constitution" rule—it is a sep-aration of powers, a check and balance. I also sign all the checks going out the door which are attached to the related invoices. As a small business, you will know virtually all your vendors of every service, thus you can spot a check headed to a strange company, individual or address. One other practice I assign to myself is categorizing our monthly credit card statement charges to appropriate general ledger accounts to prevent any potential personal use of a corporate card. The bookkeeping team does not have access to the general ledger module of our system so they cannot alter any "book" numbers nor see the aggregated financial statements and reports for an exact pic-ture of our overall financial progress.

Payroll. One area that is always challenging for a small business is payroll. Assigning this responsibility to someone other than yourself invites all manner of internal strife and chaos. Early on, I handled this myself though I did enlist the aid of our accountant to help me per-fect my own understanding. Not being able to pay your employees correctly is an inexcusable problem—to them and to the authorities. Learning this task did help me gain a quick appreciation for the total personnel cost of our company. You will appreciate the impact payroll taxes, unemployment taxes, insurance, etc. have on your bottom line and the consideration you must afford it when correctly pricing your products or services. These costs can quickly add 20% or more to the gross payroll of your employees. Eventually, I did outsource payroll and this service has provided excellent confidentiality with ready support of required detail on a person, expense or team level for general ledger tracking purposes—all at an affordable cost.

Available bookkeeping software packages have become quite effective at aggregating the array of inputs into company-prepared financial statements. When we set up our routines around our bookkeeping software, our accountants provided support to establish the level and scope of reporting we thought would be most insightful to managing the business. Off-the-shelf bookkeeping packages can be very helpful, but they certainly cannot contemplate the vast array of companies that may use them. Getting some expert advice on tailored reporting early on can be money well invested. When partnering with an accountant, it is very worthwhile to ask what information and education they provide to their clients (i.e. monthly or quarterly newsletters, e-mails or a website) so that you can continue to learn and stay abreast of any developments. At a minimum, ensure you do not fall behind on tax issues as they apply to the company, payroll and yourself.

As it relates to the company and its operations, sales tax is another area where it is worth gaining some early advice from experts in the field. If you have a national sales footprint, state sales taxes vary across the map and it is your company's responsibility to collect the appropriate amounts. If you don't, those are straight percentage points right off your after-tax bottom line margins. Additionally, your customers may also have taxable and non-taxable status. As state economies and budgets have been stressed, staying up-to-date on new taxes is a major watch item. For your business, you need to know what products and services are taxable, in what states, at what rates and when to report. Sizeable penalties await those not keeping up.

Another area where it makes imminent sense to periodically consult an accounting expert is the myriad of rules around deductibility of business expenses. Rules are constantly changing for car expenses, entertainment, etc. and you do have to keep careful records and usage logs. Add to this the tax laws around home office space or potential benefits for family members on the payroll. There are minimum requirements pertaining to what a family member must do and for how long in order to qualify for certain programs.

Finally, if you find the business struggling from a financial perspective, engaging an accountant that is familiar with your business may assist in more readily identifying some areas of your operation that are no longer performing as expected. This may help you and the team identify and address problems early or highlight where you may need to reach out for some additional external advice and consulting.

KEY TAKEAWAYS

- Financial controls are a must; separate responsibilities sufficiently to build them in

- Erroneous bookkeeping can mislead decision making and compound operational problems

- Learn how to process your payroll, the all-in cost of an employee must be appreciated to fully cost your product or service

- Get some early expert advice on creating effective financial reporting; explore available software packages

- Know how your business must collect sales taxes, and keep abreast of changes

- Don't overlook the value of engaging an outside accountant if your business is struggling, they can help pinpoint problems and inefficiencies

Memo #32
To: Dan
Re: Legal Advice

KNOCK ON WOOD, fortunately my business has not experienced a litigious history. Bearing in mind we are a distributor of customized apparel, the likelihood of that happening is low. For every small business machine shop, however, there are likely multiples of suits following employee injury or defective product claims. For every service related company, there are equally likely qualitative contractual disputes. Sadly, lawsuits have become a "way of doing business" in our economy. As you lay out your business vision and strategy, identify the vulnerable elements of your business model. Sitting down with a lawyer to discuss this set of vulnerabilities can also help you evaluate the overall potential costs of your business initiative and how that could impact pricing. At a minimum, it will highlight where you need insurance protection. Even as a distributor, we are very diligent about shoveling our walks during our Chicago winters—another task not ordinarily thought of as showing up on an entrepreneur's job description.

Seek Advice Early. When to seek legal advice should be driven by identifying when you and your business require common sense protection. I have checked in with our attorney prior to any major employee disciplinary action or firing. It protects me and it protects the company. Similarly, we have begun to create what we believe are some clever designs applied to our apparel offering so we have begun reviewing design protection via copyrights.

Depending on the type of business you operate, your need for various legal business forms will vary in amount and type. Once you get some initial legal guidance on the forms of legal protection your business requires, you should be able to create some fairly standard documentation that would no longer require an attorney to review each and every document. There are many stock legal forms available today online or from office supply chains. You should, however, at least have an initial review with your trusted attorney.

Regulatory Compliance. All companies are subject to legal and regulatory rules around the appropriate and fair treatment of workers. Gaining some legal advice upfront on the specific employment laws of your working jurisdictions is advisable. As you grow to multiple state locations, this task becomes increasingly complex.

Certain businesses are subject to greater regulatory burdens than others. For example, most dry cleaners seem to operate as small family businesses. Their business process can be prone to causing environmental damage related to the dry-cleaning processes. Where your business has any chemical processes, you should be very focused on the ability to manage waste removal in an economical and safe method. Further, you should also have insurance against any accidents.

Regulations do not just impact businesses with physical product or chemical processes. A medical products distributorship is subject to knowing all the impacts to billing for various cases involving Medicare, Medicaid, Veteran's benefits, etc. Presenting a well thought out business plan, executed per File #3 (Getting Started), to a legal advisor may very well ensure you protect your hard work against a devastating interruption caused by not following applicable regulations.

As you gain understanding of the costs of legal reviews and regulatory compliance in your business, you will have a better sense of any impact to pricing your delivered product or service.

Form of Legal Organization. Depending on your personal situation, one area worthy of gaining some helpful outside legal perspective is your company's form of organization. To be sure, this isn't just a legal issue, there are many tax, financial and operational considerations that will require some thought. Additionally, state laws may also impact some detailed considerations.

There are five basic forms of organization including:

- Sole Proprietorship
- Partnership
- Subchapter S Corporation
- Limited Liability Company (LLC)
- C Corporation

The following considerations are not meant to be exhaustive, hence the need to consult an attorney with appropriate expertise.

Sole Proprietorship—This is basically just you. No formal company structure is established and whatever inflows and outflows required for the business essentially run directly through your wallet. You still should keep separate records on the accounting of the company as the net income (or loss) is on your personal tax return. There are also some self-employment tax considerations to which you must adhere. Instances where this form of organization may be appropriate are for a "one hit wonder" invention where the hope of creating a business around it are slim, but seizing on the idea requires fast action. You are the company, so you make all the decisions. That said, should there be product liability, you are also personally responsible (including all your personal assets) for all the business' debts. Another good example could include a self-published book. In this case, the likelihood of a major liability impacting your personal worth is low.

Partnership—Similar to the Sole Proprietorship, net income flows through a partnership to the partners for inclusion on their personal tax returns. The trick about a partnership is tracking and valuing the relative contributions of each of the partners. Contributions can vary from direct capital in the form of cash, property such as office space, intellectual property like a patent, management skill as an onsite working partner, etc. Agreeing on the value of the contributions upfront is critical to establish the relative ownership the partners expect to be allocated. That ownership may also translate to voting rights depending upon your partnership agreement. The benefit of a partnership is the ability to capitalize on the strengths of each partner in forming a company. If you are lacking in a specific skill or field of expertise, forming a partnership in order to launch your complete view of your company may be the answer. Again, similar to a Sole Proprietorship, the partners are personally responsible for the debt of the partnership and each partner is responsible for the acts and omissions of their partners. As a general rule, the more partners there are in a partnership, the higher probability you encounter differing points of view on the company's direction. As the old saying goes: "too many cooks . . .."

Subchapter S Corporation—Providing a measure of personal protection from company liability begins when you consider an S Corporation. As the owners are deemed shareholders, they enjoy the same protections from individual liability as a shareholder in a C Corporation. You could create a single shareholder Sub S Corporation which may provide some tax benefits over that of a Sole Proprietorship or Partnership. S Corps also have a 100-shareholder maximum limit, but that is unlikely to be an issue for a small business. Like the prior two forms of organization, the business income (or loss) flows through to the shareholders' personal tax returns (according to their percentage ownership). Each shareholder would thus pay tax on their share of income at whatever rate their individual return mandated. Importantly, if the Sub S requires a retention of capital to address a problem or seize a growth initiative, the shareholders remain liable for tax payments on the undistributed income. This could create a personal liquidity constraint if the income from the Sub S is a shareholder's only source of income. It can also raise ownership percentage issues if some shareholders need cash and others are willing to keep it invested for growth.

Sub S Corporations do require a bit more formal administrative operational requirements, than Sole Proprietorships or Partnerships, but remain a very popular choice for small business organization. Sub S Corps are required to adopt bylaws, issue stock and hold initial and annual shareholder meetings with accompanying minutes. S Corps also have directors who elect company officers—which could be one and the same.

Limited Liability Company (LLC)—LLCs share certain attributes of S Corps including limited liability protection via a separate legal entity and pass through taxation. Importantly, strict mandates on the formal administrative requirements are less burdensome for LLCs. Transferring ownership, however, can be more burdensome as partner approval may be required.

C Corporations—For completeness of the discussion, this form of organization is generally reserved for larger companies owing to its ability to cover more complex organizational structures and business models. An entrepreneurial effort is not likely to launch as a C Corp nor be able to readily handle the upfront set-up costs.

Regardless of which form of organization you choose, there are considerations that can impact your personal economic and tax situation. For example, you will need to determine if you should be on your payroll or just take dividends. Pending your chosen legal form of organization, you should ensure you are on the payroll because your own salary, unemployment and insurance costs will become a business expense and thus won't require additional after-tax personal payments outside the company.

Further, just being on the payroll, even at a minimum salary, would qualify you for any group insurance your company may sign up to offer. At the very least, your compensation expense should be part of the cost basis for your products and services.

- Identify the potential risks inherent in your business model and visit with attorney to determine possible upfront protections

- Know the regulations to which your business is subject, penalties can be severe

- Your form of company legal organization is not just a legal formality, there are tax, financial and operational considerations

Memo #33
To: Dan
Re: Insurance and Estate Planning

WHEN THE BUZZ OF LAUNCHING THE BUSINESS is at its peak, the last thing you are going to be thinking about is "what do I need to do to retire in the style I wish?" Or "I'm young and single, why do I need insurance?" Make no mistake, you may have very solid dreams of turning the business into a veritable gold mine and living forever. Nevertheless, at some point, given the investment you make in starting your own business, you will hopefully want to be able to harvest a deserved retirement. This may mean planning a sale at some point if you do not have an appropriate heir. It may also mean financing a sale of the business through a longer-term dividend plan. Conversely, as we mentioned with crisis management (Memo #14—Crisis Management), you must prepare financially for the unexpected. There are several options to consider, all with cash and tax consequences for which you will want to have planned ahead.

Nobody wishes to think about their own mortality when they are pouring their heart and soul into building a company. The fact is, a smart risk manager, yet another hat every small business owner must wear, will think about the potential that they or a key employee could pass at an early age. Key-person life insurance is one approach. The business actually buys the policy and the proceeds could be used to stabilize the business during what would inevitably be a difficult period. Even short of death, you might think about disability insurance to cover not only income replacement, but potentially company overhead expenses, as well. Situations will most certainly vary, especially over time. Proceeds could perhaps be used to address immediate funding requirements or hire professionals to quickly come into the company to stabilize and/or manage it. As your company grows and increases in value, this risk management approach is a very wise investment for your family and estate.

For a small business owner, your personal contribution to the business in the form of your intellectual capital may be the key driver of its value. For your family's sake, with the aid of a qualified and certified financial planner, you owe your family the duty of exploring appropriate insurance plans if something were to happen to you (see Memo #14—Crisis Management). It's not a topic anyone enjoys discussing in the prime of their life, but without any level of insurance and the loss of your contribution to the business, your family could face difficult financial challenges. Additionally, without a proper will or trust coordinated through your attorney and estate planner, your family could have the business tied up in legal proceedings which could further harm its value and affect their income stream. Nearly 40% of U.S. States impose some level of estate tax and using a trust is one avenue to minimize negative impacts to the business.

As for preparing for retirement, like all workers there are avenues to provide for a comfortable retirement including the use of savings vehicles beneficial to small businesses. You will contribute to Social Security, but you can also build your private retirement accounts using various forms of Individual Retirement Accounts (IRAs) or 401(k) accounts. Simplified Employee Pension (SEP) IRAs and self-employed, or solo, 401(k) accounts provide generous annual contribution limits for small business owners. Check with a financial planner for current limits.

- Explore the use of insurance products to help protect your financial investment in your business

- Establishing a will or trust could minimize the risk to your family of value-destroying legal battles should something happen to you

- Planning for retirement is not top-of-mind when starting a business, but give early consideration to careful estate planning to maximize your retirement savings

Memo #34
To: Dan
Re: Bankers and Financing

WHEN DO YOU NEED TO CONSIDER really developing a solid relationship with a bank or financial partner? Hopefully, before it is too late as Mark Twain suggested:

> *"A banker is a fellow who lends you his umbrella when the sun is shining, but wants it back the minute it begins to rain."*

I sat on a bank board for six years and still don't rank them very highly on my critical advisor list. For small businesses that don't need to borrow from the bank, the money such companies have sitting in the bank in savings is understandably on-lent by the bank to other companies requiring capital. A cash positive company has obviously carefully managed their balance and accounts to avoid dipping below minimums, avoiding overdrafts, late payments, etc. In the current ultra-low interest rate environment, this doesn't earn that company anything in the form of interest. I suppose, fortunately enough, that describes my company today. We don't hear from our bankers; not even much on a courtesy basis. We don't earn any interest on excess balances, rather we pay our "analysis fees" for the transaction processing running through the accounts. Add to this, the Cubs won the World Series in 2016 for the first time in 108 years and we didn't get an invite to Wrigley Field the entire summer!

Educate Your Banker. If you are in need of capital to start your business or to provide for ongoing working capital financing, you need to invest time educating your banker about your business. Small business lending is usually the purview of local community banks rather than the "Wall Street" behemoths. You may or may not have a choice among bankers depending on your location. Do your homework, though, as banks and bankers develop reputations. If your conversations are solely driven by fitting you into a box based on formulas, you could be setting yourself up for a rigid relationship when the skies darken. It is not a good time to discover an overly conservative approach when you have hit your first bad stretch of profitability and require a window of patience and flexibility.

For start-up enterprises requiring some degree of funding, a community bank is likely going to be conservatively focused on some level of physical assets pledged as security for their protection. This is known as collateral. That collateral may include your own personal assets, including a personal guaranty. Within the business, owner-occupied real estate is a prime area of lending for banks. If you are a recognized brand franchisee, there may be a market-standard advance rate against the value of the franchise upon which a banker may size a loan. For an asset-laden machine shop, the required equipment may draw manufacturer or commercial finance leasing interest.

Today, there is also a rapidly growing alternative to the traditional bank. It is commonly referred to as "fintech," or financial intermediaries and financial service providers operating nearly completely off a technological platform—no bank buildings, no branches. The concept is the same as a traditional bank, facilitating the movement of cash and payments or providing investment alternatives and making loans. You will need some financial knowledge to make the best use of fintech for your company's financial needs. You won't necessarily have a consistent fintech contact to talk to if you encounter problems and the solutions are likely to be a bit more formulaic. There are new fintech providers joining the ranks every day, educate yourself to find the right solutions.

Five "C's" of Credit. Whether traditional bank or fintech, understanding what your business can afford to finance and at what cost should be part of your initial business plan as discussed in File #3 (Getting Started). To facilitate a productive banking relationship, it is worth a small investment of your time upfront. There is no guarantee you will find an experienced commercial lender that will understand the core of your business, however you can facilitate the education process by preparing an informational package about your company. You may have heard of the "5 C's of Credit," which is a rule-of-thumb template for lenders to evaluate a potential client. The first C is Character, and by having a prepared information package for a banker, you project a very positive image of a person focused on success. Okay, they'll also probe your financial history including credit reports and credit scores, but this is an easy way to demonstrate you are in command of your business.

What else might you include in this company primer? Following down the list of the other four C's is an easy guide. Capacity is your business' ability to repay any loan it may assume. Demonstrate how your business generates cash flow—in both amount and timing—sufficient to repay any borrowing requests. While a banker can only be repaid from future cash flow, demonstrating your company's cash generating history by providing a few years of historical financial statements will likely be required.

Capital is the money you have invested in the business. Your financial statements should indicate the sum total of your contribution or retained earnings. They won't, unfortunately, capture your sweat equity, but hopefully the story you relate and the proof you provide will convince them of your ability to continue to generate Capacity and Capital.

Collateral we briefly mentioned. Bankers look for a primary source of repayment of their loan, typically from some form of cash flow via earnings or sale of inventory. They understand there are multiple potential risks that come into play for each loan they extend and they try to clearly state those key risks for their underwriters and loan committees. The idea of collateral addresses a key question in a loan approval—what if those risks manifest themselves? Collateral, and its inherent value to someone else, is considered a secondary source of repayment to the bank. Collateral may also take the form of that personal guaranty if you have additional wealth outside the business.

And finally, Conditions. Highlight the purpose of the loan. How does the borrowed money facilitate the business bridging from an investment need to a period of positive cash flow? This may be due to a capital investment in equipment, real estate, inventory or maybe even an additional business acquisition. Again from File #3 (Getting Started), summarizing your business and financial strategic analysis will provide a lender the background for the considerations they will undertake in assessing how general economic conditions and competition may impact your ability to repay the loan.

Outside Investors. For some, the amount of money required for initial seed money or expansion capital requires some form of external equity capital. There are many avenues to explore here including numerous private sources such as angel investors. They tend to have a focus on the small business market as opposed to venture capitalists which focus on larger transactions. These typically affluent individuals, or angels, may provide funding individually or as part of a small group and generally will be seeking some form of equity ownership as part of the return on their capital. As such, you must ensure you have a very clear understanding how your company's performance may ultimately impact your personal equity ownership.

Similarly, angel investors will have a nearly identical focus to that of the bankers on the strategic aspects and owner commitment of a small business. An angel investor acquaintance always tells me the financial plans he reviews routinely show a rosy outlook, or the proverbial "hockey stick" profit projection. From his perspective, however, any analysis of a small business or start-up business begins with the people behind the idea. Are they credible, can they effectively sell themselves and their idea, are they worthy, do they have their own capital at risk? If not, he walks away before any review of the financials. If they clear the character hurdle, then he focuses on the business before he even considers the financial plan.

- Invest time to educate your banker, you never know when you may truly need their assistance

- The rise of fintech is providing a new generation of borrower a new generation of lender

- Understand the "5 C's of Credit" to prepare for any loan application to your banker

- The realm of equity financing requires confidence in your partners and transparency regarding the impact to your ownership equity

Memo #35
To: Dan
Re: Technology

RECALL AT THE BEGINNING OF THE BOOK I mentioned this story wasn't about international intrigue? It seems the internet has connected us all into the global "we"—whether we wanted to or not.

Since Court Products was re-launched, the internet has exploded and we are booking internet orders placed from our customers' phones at all hours of the day and night. What will the next 30 years provide in terms of a technological impact to the small business arena? This is a perfect reason to find a way to bring technological experience into your company or at least make it readily accessible. We took a quantum leap forward when my son, Dan, joined the company in 2010. He isn't a computer science major, rather he is simply a member of the tech generation. If the timing isn't right for your next generation to join, you at least need to make this a key skill factor in your ongoing hiring process.

Think back to your strategic analysis (Memo #8—Strategic Analysis) when you evaluated both your customers and your vendors—how are they using technology and how will that force your business to adapt? You have to stay ahead of these trends or risk ceding market share and profitability.

Sales. We did not have the concept of a "shopping cart" on our website until Dan came aboard and pushed it hard. How long could we have survived frustrating our customers by posting the product on the web, but forcing them to call to place an order? The fact is, as technology changes, so too are your customers. The next generations of customers are aging into your target market and you need to understand how they conduct business. It may not be like it was in the "olden days," so you and your business must pull forward to survive. Interestingly, with the shopping cart added, we saw the average dollar size of our orders decrease, but the increased volume of orders more than compensated. This single feature had clearly demonstrated we had made it easier for our customers to do business with us—that was vision alignment!

The one caveat regarding web selling, don't overreach at the start for a design award for your website. Just like our vision, we want straightforward quality service at the heart of our website. Easy to navigate, easy to order—that translates to sales. There are multiple web design services that begin with basic templates to help establish websites today. For businesses reliant on credit card sales, these payment card industry (PCI) compliant ready-to-go packages are complete with credit card information gathering capability so you don't have to worry about taking private information including card numbers and then getting hacked. The private information is automatically stored offsite in a cloud service which meets the PCI data security standards and thereby safeguarding your responsibility for a data breach. As your confidence grows regarding your customers wants and needs, so too can the bells and whistles of your website.

Prior to Dan's arrival, we made some key mistakes on my watch. To save a few dollars, we tried to design our own website from a platform that enabled a "build your own sundae" approach. While we could use our own creativity, the real value is in the underlying functionality—again, your customer must have a good experience as measured by completed sales. Our first effort looked OK, but it was already a virtual dinosaur. We started receiving the worst kind of phone calls asking "how do I place an order on the website?" Ensure you approach the review, editing and testing of your website from the customer's perspective. And, importantly, collect and think through the questions you receive—this is valuable feedback to stay relevant to your customer base.

Fulfillment/Shipping. Like other non-core competencies, creating an in-house technologically advanced shipping and tracking system is likely not going to be the best internal investment. There are readily available software programs that feed directly to UPS or USPS systems. Our program connects to our scales, calculates time in transit and costs and then prints a customer label for the best alternative. We have been able to hold down our overall employee levels based on these advancements considering we used to hand write the mailing labels and shipper logs. The improvement in accuracy also has sliced returns caused by transposed digits or poor handwriting.

For retail businesses, and even commercial manufacturers and shippers, bar code technology has greatly improved the accuracy of inventory counts and controls and point-of-sale purchases. A quick run to any larger retail store can spur your thinking about how your business can tag materials, inventory, etc. and track its usage through your business process and ultimately out the door. Connecting into smart point-of-sale terminals provides another dimension of added control. It may not prevent each theft-related occurrence, but it can alert you to investigate imbalances. The impact on our order taking and processing effort is stunning compared to when we began our business efforts 30 years ago.

Security. Technology has been great. It is creating incredible new business opportunities from Lyft to AirBnB to fintech. A Lyft driver or an owner of a few Nashville-based condos can effectively turn themselves into a small business operator using these Apps. On the flip side, news of actual or attempted massive customer data breaches, particularly among large banks or retailers, seem to be increasing in frequency. The potential pot at the end of a large company "rainbow" for a hacker seems logical, so small businesses should be spared—*right?* So I thought—*wrongly!* Hackers also know that small businesses may not have appropriately invested in the necessary level of web security and thus make easier targets. Ransomware bugs actually may not know how big (or small) their target is.

As noted earlier, I like to ensure we keep our vendors happy and I received a courteously-worded past due e-mail notice from one vendor with an attached copy of the invoice. I opened the invoice and nothing happened—other than a sinking feeling in my stomach. Two weeks passed (while presumably the ransomware corrupted our system) and then WHAM—we were totally locked out of our system and files.

We had two options. One was to reload our software, restore via backups and hope we had everything as current as possible. This takes a good bit of time and resource for a small business and we would have to re-load all data since our last backup. The second alternative was to pay the ransom and get our files back immediately. After some outside consultation with two technology consultants that advised us to pay, we did opt to pay the ransom. The theory is you should expect to get your information back because if the hackers didn't release it, word gets out and no future targets would attempt to pay the demanded ransoms.

We scrambled over a weekend to open a bitcoin account as the ransom was to double every 72 hours. To our surprise, it took about four days to open the account in a cost-effective manner. A "premium" approach is available, but that would effectively just increase our ransom. Bitcoin purchased (at $600 per), we paid the ransom and waited for the code to unlock the files. The ransom was not a large amount. The theory being most targets subsequently don't bother to report the theft and the hackers continue to move on to the next victims.

The worst part of the whole episode was this comment embedded in the ransom payment instructions:

> "The reason we are doing this is to show you how vulnerable the internet is and hopefully with your help we can build a safer and more secure internet!"

Now, talk about rubbing salt in a fresh wound! When it was all over, we went through a very thorough review and upgrade of our security and our backup procedures. We also made a point of investing more in arranging to have a technology service on retainer for emergency or complex problems. As part of your strategic planning, including a technology security review every so often would be a very wise operational insurance policy. We are now able to store frequent pictures of our programs, files and data on our cloud service provider so everything can be restored in one action rather than wiping the system clean, restoring the backup and re-loading data from the last backup. This was a tough lesson to learn to ensure we are now prepared for today's networking environment.

The cost to address a cyber theft has many hard dollar charges in the form of updated software (and maybe a ransom). Think, however, about the cost to our business as we were all consumed by the breach, we lost sales, we lost profit, we operated inefficiently. The costs can be substantial. If you were to have a customer data breach, think of the cost of all the goodwill lost. Prevention is well worth the cost.

KEY TAKEAWAYS

- Plan to make technology knowledge a skill factor in your ongoing hiring plan

- Know how your customers and vendors are using technology and how it is apt to impact your business

- Review your technology interface from your customers' perspective, not yours

- An annual review of your technology security should be part of your strategic plan

Memo #36
To: Dan
Re: Board of Advisors/Mentors

AS YOU REFLECT BACK ON THE MYRIAD of strategic and tactical efforts to start and build a small business enterprise, the notion of reaching out for some guidance along the way is natural. For a younger business person without a wealth of experience, it is highly recommended. Even once you have your business up and running and feel proud of the progress you have made, the challenge of staying ahead of the competition requires you to stay at the forefront of evolving trends and issues related to your business. A valuable source of input on such trends and issues can be gained through creating some form of a board of advisors, even if a rather informal network.

Effective Advisory. The goal of forming an advisory board is to have yourself and your decision-making challenged and your intractable problems debated. It should not solely be about seeking external validation. And, it definitely should not be about seeking answers— you are the decision maker. To achieve an effective advisory board, you will need to find a group willing to be open and honest with you and positive about building your business. For them to deliver valued advice and counsel, however, you also must be totally open and honest with them. You cannot expect outsiders to be effective advisors without having access to the necessary information on your business.

There are three different approaches you could consider. First, depending upon your location, there may be many organizations you could join that bring together small business owners in a discussion group format. Essentially, a franchisee/coordinator of one of these organizations reaches out to small business executives to form a group that periodically gathers to discuss emerging trends and issues. The group becomes a quasi-board for each other's business. In addition, the group members have the opportunity to lay out individual concerns and seek feedback from others' personal experience or knowledge set. Effectively, it is hopefully pulling together like-minded business owners to pool knowledge and share for the common good. These organizations do charge a fee to join and can become a solid source of experience on a vast range of issues. Some of the drawbacks include 1) the generality of some of the discussion may not be an effective use of your time; 2) some members could monopolize the sessions or there may not be enough time for each member to get their own agenda discussed each meeting; 3) there is no guaranty of the continuity of the group members or the coordinator which could stifle longer term effectiveness; and 4) you need to have confidence your group will embrace confidentiality.

The second approach, forming a formal board of advisors, can solve some of the drawbacks of the first approach. You may have to figure out, however, what the overall cost might entail. Hosting effective meetings of a Board will be greatly enhanced by: 1) meticulous preparation and selection of materials; 2) organized and appropriately forceful discussion leadership and moderating; 3) some form of quid-pro-quo compensation, maybe not cash, but perhaps a reciprocal consult; and, of course 4) patient coordination of busy schedules. In addition, be clear upfront what the expectations are for the advisory members, i.e. monthly/quarterly calls and/or meetings.

With Court Products, we had a phase where we had stagnated a bit in terms of growth and new initiatives. Having had my father-in-law as a company founder, I tapped some of his experienced and accomplished business contacts with small business experience to form my own advisory board. I gathered an investment counselor who raised capital for owners of small businesses through his clientele, an executive that had navigated a successful business turnaround and an accountant. I then prepared my first presentation complete with company history, financials and discussion of future goals. The group asked a lot of good and pointed questions on the current market, how we operated and my personal goals. At the end of this, my first 3-hour advisory board meeting, the consensus was: "your growth is limited—sell the business!" That was my first and last meeting with this "Board!"

The third approach, presuming you have the commitment to stick with it, is to create a network of experienced and trusted advisors through your own friends, acquaintances and business colleagues. I also view this approach as a "Board of Mentors." While the cost can be managed, you will need a solid commitment to routinely insert into your schedule the appropriate number of one-off lunches, coffees and other meetings. To properly set expectations, it would be best to alert these people to your intentions, otherwise after a couple of grillings over a sandwich, your advisor may come away with a distinctly poor impression. Your success will be enhanced if you are able to serve a beneficial purpose for their own endeavors. That is, ensuring the give and take is a two-way exchange. You might also find some retired individuals who would appreciate the intellectual challenge of working through your current thought list. Be cautious of selecting close friends, you may not get the objectivity you seek—and need. Another drawback of this approach is you would not necessarily afford the chosen group of advisors to hear the same consistent story and allow them to feed off each other in an effort to help pull apart and solve a particular issue.

Other Advisors. Blurring the line of advisors, I also use my vendors as a resource for industry trends and developments. This borders on basic attention to everyday business operations and strategy, but you may find you develop some very strong bonds with certain vendors that go beyond a commercial relationship. I will pick my vendors' brains for what they are hearing from their vendors and other customers. Maybe some segment of the market is selling a hot new product and with a little thought and planning, we could too. In a distribution business, this "advisory" information is important to effectively managing inventory. There are examples of invested parties holding representation on big company boards, think of the United Auto Workers on the Board of the then Big Three (GM, Ford, Chrysler). For a small business, the impact of a key vendor having a direct line of sight to your financials is a non-starter. Other "advisors" you could tap include some of your professional resources including accountants, lawyers or employment agencies.

An example of a vendor that has become a very good friend and important advisor was one of my early partners on the paper catalogue. During those years, we would start with a photographer, then a designer and then go off to the printer. Three different partners, three different viewpoints on what we were creating, three different timetables. It became a time suck. We were able to locate a company that could do it all, A to Z. This one-stop shopping not only accelerated the development timeline, it greatly improved the step-to-step coordination enabling us to get to the best finished product possible because they had a better understanding of our overall goal. As the relationship developed, they would introduce new approaches that kept moving the overall quality of the finished product to a more professional style. This business partner, Gary, knows our business very well. He has consistently demonstrated that he thinks about what will serve Court Products best and brings us excellent ideas. We may not take up each idea, but it shows you can develop a relationship with a partner that not only is of mutual economic benefit, but it is also founded on a principle of being a valued advisor. Maybe that is their vision!

KEY TAKEAWAYS

- Seeking guidance from experienced people outside your company demonstrates your business confidence and maturity

- Consistency is key—share timely information, be clear in your guidance requests, and thank them for the invaluable perspective

- Boards should challenge you and help you debate more complex business issues, not make final decisions

- Formal advisory boards require time and some hard costs; their fiduciary responsibility can only be met by your willingness and ability to share information

- Consider forging appropriately bounded advisory relationships with strong vendors, they will know your business from an important perspective

Memo #37
To: Dan
Re: Real Estate and Premises Manager

ONE AREA OF COST MANAGEMENT FOR SMALL BUSINESSES is that of the physical office, manufacturing, warehousing or visitor space. Where possible, I highly recommend you seek your own separated and locked space, rather than a shared-space/shared-cost arrangement. I offer this advice despite the fact shared office space leases are a significant new real estate market trend. The potential for leaked information via physical or verbal means is very high. Customer confidentiality could be easily compromised and lead to significant negative business consequences. For any business with a physical product, the ability to satisfactorily manage quality, safety or theft becomes challenged. Overall, multiple business purposes and goals of more than one company in one space do not add up to an efficient and effective operation.

Leasing versus buying your physical premises is impacted by a multitude of factors including your needs to be close to customers, vendors, transportation, etc. Add to this your own capital availability as well as the "local" market for available space that fits—and accepts—your business purpose and you suddenly have a multi-pronged decision tree to evaluate. Using an analysis similar to a discounted cash flow (Memo #9—Financial Analysis) can help you evaluate the economic benefit of lease vs. buy. Essentially, you are comparing a rent stream over time to ownership costs including upfront acquisition costs, taxes, insurance and maintenance.

Regardless of your lease/buy decision, you will be a premises manager and you will inevitably receive the 2 a.m. phone calls that your alarms have been activated. Having not yet learned the lesson of having our own space, I was awakened in the early morning hours by our alarm service. The police also received the call and thankfully were there before my 30-minute drive time. In fact, not having found anything, the police left before I arrived. I parked out front with my high-beam headlights plastered to the front windows. Nothing rattles your nerves more than checking out a dark business premise at two in the morning. As I made my checks, I noticed our "office neighbor" had stacked shrink-wrapped pallets 3-high. Up toward the top, where one of the wraps had loosened, the air current from the HVAC vents would blow and subsequently activate our warehouse motion detectors. The other company, however, didn't obviously feel the need to answer the 2 a.m. call!

KEY TAKEAWAYS

- Lease vs. buy analysis is not just financial, there are many non-monetary considerations

- Shared office space is a growing trend; understand your ability to protect confidential and proprietary information

Memo #38
To: Dan
Re: Employment Service Agencies

DEPENDING ON YOUR FREQUENCY OF HAVING TO FIND new employees, an employment service can be very helpful if you invest some time to develop a relationship. If they are able to get to know your business, they can better screen appropriate candidates and make your hiring process much more efficient. They can assist in writing help wanted ads that carefully convey your desired applicant's skillset in a language the ad-reader will understand.

A good service will also be able to inform you on the market for certain skills, salary ranges, etc. As noted, they are also a good source for educating you and your team on appropriate and effective interviewing strategies as well as guiding you toward completion of a comprehensive employee manual. Along the same lines, they can provide you some "legal guidance" in terms of topics you can and cannot introduce during the interview process.

KEY TAKEAWAYS

- To be a valuable source for market knowledge, let the agency get to know you

- Agencies are more than a source for the next hire

File #8

& Son (or Daughter)

Memo #39
To: Dan
Re: More Than Passing the Keys

AS A YOUNG ENTREPRENEUR juggling the many requirements of a new business, it is a virtual certainty the last thing you will be thinking about is succession and retirement. But, for those young entrepreneurs that start building a family, the arrival of a newborn might suddenly start you thinking about the exciting day you could be in business with a next generation! Conversely, maybe you are thinking about joining your family's small business. This book has primarily addressed the considerations of potential or actual new business owners. With hard work, you will also begin to encounter the issues confronting seasoned small business owners—including succession.

One question the seasoned small business owner needs to ask themselves after introducing a next generation and actually seeing them capably take the reins is "when is the right time to really GO?" And then, not come back the following Monday morning! OK, you will likely be around as the Chairman Emeritus at family dinners for many years to come. Nevertheless, there will be many deeply personal questions that need to be probed to answer this question for you and clearly a "one size" answer will not fit all. Do you need to sell the business so you will have retirement savings? Would you benefit from an ongoing ownership dividend or would you envision financing the sale over time? Can you pass the business on to your next generation in a way that won't create family disharmony and risk upending the success of the company? Are there special tax considerations that should influence how the business is passed along and over what time period? It is worth consulting an estate planner (Memo #33—Estate Planning) well before this actual day as some actions may require a much earlier start.

Personally, I grew up amidst modest means; I mentioned my Dad was a teacher. We didn't vacation to fancy hotel resorts, we camped our way across the U.S. and the outdoors was our resort. We measured our wealth by the size of our campfire woodpile—and we were RICH, because we worked hard for it! The point of this being—as mentioned early on—Court Products truly is not that next groundbreaking internet app. Be proud if you are able to create a business that provides a comfortable living over your personal career. Be even prouder you provided an opportunity for others to improve their standard of living. Just as with any other worker in any other company where they are not the owner, you too should have been saving over the years in order to provide in some way for your retirement. Planning for your complete retirement nest egg to come from the value of your company upon sale at your retirement date is a very risky gambit, particularly if you are the main driver of the business' value.

We discussed the impact on your employees of a number of issues that may arise during your company's history (File #6—CEO of HR; Every Day!). As noted, in a small business, everyone will end up knowing a good bit about each other's personal situations, including family members. For the owner, there is essentially a free pass to integrate his family into the business over time. Sometimes this begins early via some summer work experiences or sometimes it comes later after a "young adult" has gone out and worked on their own for a few years and ultimately decides to come and join the small family business. Either way, at some point you may need to address the level of potential resentment from other employees toward entitlement afforded the adult child of a small business owner.

Of course, many times there may not be a next generation of the owner to step in and assume the leadership role. In this case, you have a couple of options. In one instance, you can decide to sell the business at the point you decide you are ready to move on to other pursuits. Challenges might include timing. Are you able to sell at a value near the top of your industry's cycle? Of course, finding an interested buyer willing to pay what you think the business is worth may also be tough. Alternatively, you might wish to thoughtfully think through how you can bring in a truly interested heir apparent, or outside successor, and work out a transition, including a buyout agreement. This period provides you the opportunity to coach this person and let them learn the business and your business contacts so that the value of the company doesn't walk out with you. Since you are keeping your capital in the business, you are trusting this person to maintain the company with sufficient financial capacity to continue to make your earn-out payments. Choose wisely. The best answer may not be the most obvious one.

KEY TAKEAWAYS

- Transition is not a one-day handover; care must be taken to decide how long the transition should last

- Your Estate Planning should raise some of the when and how questions ahead of the actual event

- The process will likely differ between an adult child heir, a chosen successor or an outright sale

Memo #40
To: Dan
Re: Signs You are Ready to Pass the Baton

THE YEARS OF EFFORT AND TOIL INVESTED in building a business make it very hard to say "goodbye." Like many things in life, when to make this call involves a multitude of factors, it is not a simple binary choice—in or out. On the positive side, your business has flourished and your good fortune has allowed you to work less and play more. At the other end, consider the possibility of a life-threatening health issue that forces you to scale back, or even stop, working. In either of these cases, you'll know the signs—though health issues can arise suddenly and force a suboptimal decision timeline.

Interpret the Signs. At that positive end, having had a fortunate run in your business is a great thing. You created a thriving business, certainly susceptible to some ups and downs, but something that has provided you the opportunity to enjoy more free time or a retirement with the ability to pass along a living business legacy to your kids. Perhaps you have developed a passion to contribute your time in a more substantive way to any number of charitable organizations. Or, maybe your thoughts are that you want to travel at a time you can still physically enjoy seeing and experiencing the world. In addition to my woodshop I have set up back in the warehouse, I began pursuing another longshot hobby I had pondered for decades—learning to play the guitar. Other than owning a stereo, music was never a big part of my life—though my college roommates may wish to differ as I jammed on my tennis racquet to B.T.O.'s "Taking Care of Business" (talk about irony!). One can read these signs as achieving greater personal productivity. On the other hand, be honest and ensure they are not reactions to boredom with your role because that may impact your business and its value.

That other end of the spectrum where a health issue arises can be very demoralizing. In fact, maybe it is not even you, it could be your spouse, a child or maybe even a parent that draws your time and attention away from your business where you are the lead actor every day. For health issues, it can be very difficult to come to terms emotionally with the fact that your ability to commit the necessary time and energy to your business may never come back to what you could give previously. This is a very difficult issue to firmly determine and make the tough call to transition to some other leadership arrangement.

Across this spectrum, there are many other signs or considerations that begin to trigger your thinking about transitioning out of your business. Maybe you have hit the age your parents retired, your friends or siblings are retiring, your eligibility for social security—the list goes on. What is important is that you not overreact to these initial triggers, rather you use them to begin thoughtfully planning how your exit can provide an enjoyable transition and preserve the value of the business you created.

Other than the omens you begin to read personally, sometimes you may find more overt signals coming from your "field of experts." Perhaps your accountant or attorney begins questioning you about plans for succession before any of those other "omen" have appeared. These professionals have a window into many companies and for all the stories that work out well, they see their fair share of those people who have been caught off guard. My accountant happened to raise the issue to me when I was 54 years old which really caught me off guard. I was still of the mindset that retiring was something only "old people" should be thinking about.

As noted, the most difficult sign to effectively deal with is the one you don't—or refuse—to read. That is the one where your personal motivation has waned and you are not giving your all to the business. Are you arriving later, leaving earlier, passing up growth opportunities? Has your spouse reflected back that you seem unhappy and agitated about your daily business challenges? In this case, the value of your years of investment can begin deteriorating sharply in a short period of time. The atmosphere within your business among your teammates will also become a telltale sign. Maintaining an honest assessment of the reviews of your business' performance is critical. If the driving force for poor performance is your lack of engagement, you must be able to make the call as to whether you can get that motivation back or whether you should begin to think about transitioning out of the business entirely.

Emotionally Retiring. One aspect of being prepared to step away that you really won't be able to measure, but for the passage of time, is whether you can emotionally separate what you believe is your "legacy" from what your child may end up evolving the business to be. Note, I did not say "evolving with your company" because upon transition, it is theirs to run. There are some areas in which I readily see Dan making his own mark, specifically regarding technology. I have accepted this reality. The next generations are just more comfortable and more attuned to what is available, how it is used and how to take advantage. A slight derivative to this is just the general tastes, fads and preferences of each generation. It is important in our business to stay relevant given apparel can go out of style. But any business must be prepared to adapt to changing preferences for fashion, diets, architectural styles, industry innovations, etc. Just being younger won't guarantee anything, they have to be committed to learn the industry. Right now, I see Dan's increasing influence on the company and it is one of those important signs I read (present tense!) for my own retirement decision.

Philosophically, the toughest aspect of stepping away is missing out on that next big change in the business. My adventurous nature includes hiking with my daughter in the mountains of Colorado and

Wyoming. "Bagging 14ers" means climbing peaks in excess of 14,000 feet and Colorado has just over 50. My wife thinks we are crazy and has asked "why do you like to do that?" My answer has always been the same—you never know what you might see over the next ridge, around the next outcrop, or from the very top. There could be a beautiful mountain lake, a herd of wildlife nurturing their young in the summer sun, a panorama to take your breath away—whatever it may be, I don't want to miss out on it. That is the same reason I will have a tough time totally disengaging from the business. I'd love to see the next big advancement Dan comes up with, whether it be a new product line, a technological advance, who could really know? I'd just like to be there to see it and experience it as it plays out—not just hear about it over dinner.

KEY TAKEAWAYS

- Be honest whether a late career desire to take more personal time is reflective of success or boredom; the latter could ruin your business

- As you begin to read signs about possibly retiring, don't overreact, plan thoughtfully

- As you set out a transition plan, be as complete as possible with goals and timelines

- Assuming you sold the company, recognize upon your exit, you have to learn to "let go," it is no longer your living legacy

Memo #41
To: Dan
Re: Initial Training for the Family Member

IN GENERAL, HAVING YOUR TEAM UNDERSTAND that one or more of your adult children are going to join the business should not come as a complete shock. As mentioned, in a small office, you will all know pretty much about each other's personal situation—including the boss'. There may be summers of work for your children along the way and there likely should be some planning during routine staff meetings about others joining the company, including adult children of the boss.

There is no "best" way to bring an adult child into the business. In many cases, it will depend on their age, experience and educational background. Just because your kid graduated with an art history major does not mean they cannot learn the range of skills that can make them successful in your business. That is, presuming your business is not a professional practice requiring some form of licensing such as an accountant, lawyer, architect, etc.

In other cases, perhaps you have an adult child who is seeking some level of experience in a business environment, but candidly is not interested in the family business as a career path. Bringing aboard a child for a couple of years as preparation for a graduate business degree may also be a rewarding and happy experience for both of you.

A Career Plan. When one of your adult children joins the company, it can be helpful to create a "career plan" whether or not you know the longer term nature of their involvement. In the case where they are joining with every intention of staying, you need to be able to evaluate their execution of their daily roles and responsibilities just as you would with any other employee. In small businesses, your business' success depends on everyone pulling their weight—the boss' offspring included!

In Dan's case, the economy was mired in the Great Recession when he graduated from college in 2010. Court Products was a safe port in the midst of the storm. He came aboard with the intent to think through what truly interested him and gain some experience along the way. I confess, I didn't draw up the guidelines and expectations I discussed since we discussed the "interim" nature of the role when he came aboard. That said, however, my lesson learned is that time flies, especially when you are pouring your all into a business during a massive recession and technology is seemingly forcing you to change your approach on a daily basis. As each wave of the storm has crashed over us, we have developed a strong partnership and I have been exceptionally fortunate to have him develop a passion for the business equal to my own.

I had two main objectives as Dan came into the business. First, it was important to demonstrate to the existing team that he was not being granted a free ride. He was going to have to demonstrate he could learn the good with the bad—which very much included his own shift at cleaning the toilets! He was not going to be able to come in and select what he wanted to do and in what order. I was determined that he learn the business from the ground up.

The second objective was to help him learn how to listen to the customer, appreciate the customer and read the customer. There may be a tendency for young folks to think they can place themselves in someone else's shoes and assume they can then read their mind. It doesn't work that way. A customer base is filled with as many different preferences as there are customers and one person cannot pretend to read them all perfectly.

Training Example. Dan started in our production and warehouse area. Preparing and storing, then picking, packing and shipping to ensure our customer's main concern, fast and accurate order delivery, was addressed. Just as on a manufacturing plant floor, our distribution warehouse is where the customer's demand is being fulfilled. There is no better place to visually appreciate this phase of the order and "paper" flow of the business. Knowing this process also plants the seeds of appreciation for any changes to strategy that may impact this function. A new line to new customers requires different space, perhaps different packaging driving different costs. Even in a service business, a new service requires new skills, meaning training or hiring new people. Likewise in manufacturing, adding a new product could disrupt the efficiently planned flow of materials around a plant floor and drive up costs. Driving strategy and change requires an appreciation of the basic support processes that must come together to preserve your company's bottom line.

Warehouse appreciation demonstrated, he joined our administrative office in a desk out on the floor like everybody else. There was no private cubicle or office waiting. Sitting amidst the team that handles customer service, order taking, returns/exchanges, etc. was the best way for him to learn different interpersonal styles from his own teammates. He would also come to appreciate that even in a small business, the need to reach out to your fellow teammates and bounce ideas and questions is critical for the success and growth of the company. This particular role within Court Products is the nexus of the team. Therefore, it demonstrated to the entire group that Dan was expected to learn this business by pulling his own weight and completing his fair share of the "to do" pile.

We then moved on to the bookkeeping responsibilities and this rounded out the knowledge set to complete all the day-to-day duties across the team. He was also then ready to fill in should anyone be on vacation or out ill. I actually fed him to the wolves at year-end his first year when my wife and I visited our daughter in Thailand while she was completing a semester abroad. Dan had to complete the year-end accounting and close the books with the accountants.

With the relatively short-term day-to-day baptism complete, the next challenge was a longer-term plan to position him in my role as the "go to" for the rest of the team. To do this, he became a key participant/ leader in our strategic planning initiatives. During his third year at the company, we had Dan participate in the weekly meeting agenda setting as well as taking point on certain topics. This provided him the platform to delegate or provide direction on special projects that we had discussed. Importantly, this positioned him to work directly with the team instead of through me.

Throughout his indoctrination into the day-to-day roles, Dan brought to our team a natural interest in technology. Very nearly from day one, he began investigating the most effective use of the web for a business like Court Products. By his fifth year, along with his website development, Dan took the sole lead on our annual catalogue strategy.

Throughout this process, it is important not to try to hide the true objective from the team. This family member is in the company to learn the business and hopefully assume leadership one day. There is nothing wrong with some very public commentary to the team that they should expect your child, over time, to prove themselves worthy and deserving of moving into a #2 role and ultimately the #1 role in the company. Such advancement need not be expected as a given, but the execution of the plan should also not be left purposefully unstated. Give your team credit, they will have figured that out and any lack of transparency will be damaging for morale.

Working with Customers and Vendors. Training and mentoring with your external constituencies may require a bit of a different approach. Your vendors and customers are not likely to be immediately impacted by your child's presence. With our customer base, and similar to others where the number of customers far outweighs the customer service team, their knowledge of our team is typically only a first name basis. Among our team, thankfully, we don't have any duplicate first names. So, if a person calls and follows up with Dan, he gets Dan. He doesn't necessarily know he is Dan Stetson, son of the President. Frankly, several years in and this fact carries on just the same today. Anonymity can be a blessing as your child learns the business on the customer side. If it can't be protected because you have much more formal customer relationships, you may have to manage the volume of customers that are trying to position their dialogue with the owner's family member. There is no point overwhelming your child and setting them up for disappointment because they cannot handle the flood of customer inquiries, projects, etc. Either way, the goal is that any customer gets top of the line service from any teammate—founding family member or not.

As for our vendors, given our goal of creating long term relationships, some of our best were very aware of my family. Where that wasn't the case, Dan assumed point so that there wasn't a hint of any special treatment. Where I might also be involved in some follow up, it was enlightening to have a rep make comments about prior meetings with Dan. It made for a good feedback mechanism. Maybe a bit disingenuous toward the rep, but remaining mum was far from a malicious undertaking on my part. For the astute reps visiting me in my office, maybe the family pictures in my office eventually tipped them off! As an aside, one thing we learned along the way about our really good vendors was that they would take it upon themselves to help educate Dan on various issues as they foresaw the day he might be calling all the shots. I value that long-term relationship approach.

Create Real Test Runs. As a dry run on a business initiative, Dan and I generated the concept of the previously mentioned Alpine Way product line. It didn't directly impact our core product line and customer base, so we set it up as a separate stand-alone company and EACH put our own financial skin in the game—which we lost. It has been a great learning experience on many related facets of our core business while not impacting the existing company or its infrastructure. With an investment of his own in a fairly small application, Dan learned to pay attention to the full range of strategic, management and operational decisions. His appreciation for what it has taken to launch and operate Court Products was greatly enhanced and it reinforced the highly-valued understanding of the "know your market" mantra. You don't need to experiment with a full line product or service extension. Try delegating significant project initiatives or process changes.

Late-Transition Considerations. A few areas Dan has yet to fully engage in are running point on HR and acting as the interface to the external professionals in accounting and legal. As I am still generally in the office on a daily basis, actively involved in the execution of our strategies—and, by the way, still own the company—I haven't removed myself as the one writing the appraisals. I view this not only as current cover for Dan's focus and development in other operational areas, but also a continued sense of comfort for the rest of the team. The year-end accounting and legal aspects of our Sub S structure may be considered a bit mundane, but they are very important in fulfilling an understanding of capital and administrative management. Seeing as this remains my investment, it made sense to hold this one to the end where we may begin a discussion about his investment desires.

KEY TAKEAWAYS

- Where possible, have your child learn the business from the ground up, even the most menial of tasks

- Learning each of the roles will make your child appreciate the impact of forced vs. elective change

- The training process of your child should be visible to the team, they will respect the knowledge was gained with hard work

- Where possible, delegate actual project initiatives to challenge planning, selling and implementation

Memo #42
To: Dan
Re: Is Your Adult Child Ready to "Step Up?"

ONCE ONE OR A MORE OF YOUR ADULT CHILDREN have successfully learned the business and positively contributed to its success, your thoughts will eventually turn toward possible leadership succession. The next big question becomes, however, whether any of your adult children are interested and prepared to assume the mantle of leadership the company requires. As the saying goes, timing is everything. It is not just knowing what needs to be done along with the how and when; it is whether they have the willingness, skill and aptitude to execute. If they are not quite ready, you should focus on specific steps to mentor their leadership attributes.

Mentoring Program. Your training effort should already have provided relevant experiences of sufficient duration to learn and understand the various roles across the business. Now, you must ensure you are not just leading up to a day where you drop your remaining responsibilities on top of what you had already been giving them. You will need to carefully work together to ensure that as you begin transitioning your responsibilities, your son or daughter has the opportunity to transition some of their current responsibilities to others, including a new hire if necessary. It is not a badge or a nameplate you are handing over, it is a full deck of time-consuming, thought-provoking critical roles and responsibilities that drive the day-to-day and long-term success of your company.

One approach to avoiding such a misstep is to draw up some guidelines and expectations of progress as you formally recognize the idea of an adult child stepping in to the leadership role. Both of you will know the expectations for yourself and each other and you should be able to measure your progress against these guidelines. Make an effort to periodically review progress and make appropriate adjustments so as to avoid getting off track in a way that could end up down a path of mutual disappointment and family strife.

Dan and I have now had several years shoulder-to-shoulder to share in how the operations of the business work. Importantly, we have had some crisis management opportunities to learn to handle the unexpected. Not that the same crises will arise again, but situation management and the requirement for a steady leadership influence on our teammates are skills that require some practice.

Where I began to notice Dan's potential to step up to more responsibility, even leading the company, was the gradual tapering off of the number of times he came to me to ask specific or even philosophical questions about the business. He developed a good day-to-day feel for what worked and what did not, and he listened to my historical recollections of what worked and what had not. He also was listening to the team and developed his own rapport. That skill serves as the best information gathering system a small business leader can create. Had he not been asking questions along the way, that would have been a red flag to me signifying his heart wasn't into pursuing a longer-term career within Court Products.

As difficult as it is to say, even with a full-time adult child in your business, you need to sometimes think of "appraising" them just as you would any other teammate. As you consider the personal factors that drive success in your business (recall File #2—Is Small Business Right for You?), ask yourself as honestly as you can whether you think your son or daughter possesses or is developing those traits and skills. Some can be rather overt, some much more subtle. As a physically-active recent college grad attuned to today's oversaturated ad-based society, Dan has demonstrated maturity in his business thinking around inventory selection. He is not buying for himself. And, at times, he is likely marketing to a demographic that could be twice his age. We can't survive hoping our customers like our taste, we need to know what drives theirs.

Is the Team Ready? Transitioning leadership of the business to a child is not just a decision about their skills and readiness. Your team must also be up to the challenge and today we have a tremendous group where each knows their roles. They get their work done efficiently and effectively and they pitch in when and where needed. Frankly, even with Dan's current level of preparedness, I am not certain we could pull off a complete transition were we to have had some of our previous crews in place. Our current team is an incredibly diligent and cohesive group of employees that would enable Dan to step in today and confidently stay the course. The strength of your team can be as important as the preparedness of your child.

Dan started in on the absolute ground floor as mentioned. To them, the entire notion of Dan initially joining the company was just another set of hands for the team. The lesson here is that even if transitioning to an adult child, the longer you can make that transition period, the easier it is on the rest of the team to ease into the change.

One of the most critical, and visible, signs your adult child is ready occurs when you observe the team actually approaching your son or daughter with their questions or thoughts. It may be a bit of a shock to you at first, but realize that this is a hugely positive sign that your adult child is earning the respect of the team. That respect is essential to providing the longer term leadership the business will require. Maybe it is the reality of your team seeing "the writing on the wall," but take a moment to relish that you have actually created and executed an effective transition plan.

Hard Questions. What if you determine your child is not ready? Did you not prepare them properly or did you misjudge their interest and/or ability? If your estate planning is dependent around an earn-out over time, will the business survive in order to realize your full payout? Candidly, some of us can be guilty to some degree of judging our own children with those proverbial rose-colored glasses.

Now to flip the script, what if you have flawlessly executed your role as mentor, but you seem to be rethinking your decision to actually disengage from the business. Your adult child could start feeling frustration about their inability to truly run the show and this may prompt them to re-think their career choice or become disruptive within the company. Bear in mind, people tend to move on to businesses and industries they know well. Your child could show up at a competitor—or worse, as a competitor! Yet another sad result, you could end up feeling you need to fire your child. I've seen both—it can and does happen. Even in a small office, sides can be drawn up as an adult child attempts to gather support among some employees. It is not a healthy atmosphere. Peace at the holiday dinner table is one good reason to avoid these outcomes; another is peace within your office.

Another difficult question we've touched on is the topic of a potential health scare impacting an owner's continued ability to effectively run the company. The thought of what we would do has, on occasion, entered my mind. Like the vast majority of reasonably healthy busy people, however, I confess to not doing anything about it. Why do I bring this up again now? Well, what if you have created this valuable enterprise and now you need it to continue to provide for your family but neither you nor anyone else in the family can provide the leadership and direction the company requires. Alternatively, maybe your adult children are not quite of the age, experience or mindset to step into the demands and pressure of leading a small business.

At this point, a search for a capable, and available, executive becomes a difficult balancing act. You would want to find someone committed to preserving your vision; however, most of these capable executives might be looking for something they can eventually call their own. This could leave you wondering how long the arrangement may last. Unfortunately, there are no guarantees on any employee's tenure. Working through your own network of business contacts or through an employment agency may help you find executives in search of shorter term transition roles, maybe bringing a retired "CEO" back to active duty. Using a specific recruiting firm can get rather expensive for a small business budget. If you have insured yourself against a long-term disability, insurance proceeds might help fund this search. You must find the balance between these costs and the preservation of your company's value.

I will add a post script here and it is purposefully not beginning the thought with "finally." You are the one that needs to be confident in making the call as to whether one of your adult children is prepared to officially take over. That said, I know our plan seems to be working because Dan is encouraging me to take more time away from the office whether for my workouts, my workshop or travelling with my wife. It could be read that he wants me out of the way, but our working relationship suggests it is a solid showing of the confidence we have built in his ability to run the office. Either way, it's a good sign to me that he wants to do it and he can handle it.

KEY TAKEAWAYS

- Transitioning is not about handing over an office nameplate; it is a demanding full-time job

- A thoughtful, written transition plan with expectations and timelines should form the basis for open dialogue during your leadership transition process

- Be confident of your adult child's engagement in the business and respect from the team; both must be readily apparent to create an effective transition

- Review the strengths and needs of your current team at the time of transition; addressing those needs should be part of the transition plan

- If your son or daughter is not ready, consider a search for an interim executive

Memo #43
To: Dan
Re: What if it is "& Son & Daughter & ...?"

THERE ARE COUNTLESS SMALL BUSINESS OWNERS that may have some difficult family decisions to make as they think about introducing their kids into the business. As mentioned, I also have a daughter. She is two years younger than her brother Dan and works in wildlife management. At this point, she remains dedicated to her chosen environmental and natural resources interests.

There are two areas that require your consideration when you have more than one child. First, is there room for more than one in the company? Follow on questions include: if not, who gets it and if so, who does what? The second consideration is, if you don't have all the children involved, how do you equitably divide your estate which includes the company?

A Role for How Many? On the first issue, you could get lucky and have some of your children pursue other career paths aligned to their particular interests. If you are running a community real estate agency and your child wants to be a doctor, it is clear they will bypass your profession. Also lucky are those that might have the ability to take on more than one child because the business is expandable much like a real estate or an insurance agency—new agents are tasked with sourcing their own leads and demonstrating their skills. In businesses where that scalable opportunity may not exist, it remains your role to hire the right people and your process should not waiver terribly from how you have built your company. Assess each child's strengths and weaknesses, match them to appropriate responsibilities, train and mentor them toward proficiency and evaluate them with honesty. From birth, you know your kids have differing skills, personalities and goals, and these will impact your business in different ways.

A challenge with having more than one child in the business is that as time passes and each child hopefully wishes to continue to improve upon their skills and careers, the pyramid atop the company narrows. As early in their careers as possible, you should honestly and openly articulate the relative value of each child's contributions so that a cataclysmic family blowout does not occur over some surprise leadership announcement. Happy stories exist of smoothly operating multi-generational family businesses. Unfortunately, there are likely as many where jealousies and viewpoints of unfair play either destroyed the business or destroyed the family. As mentioned relative to providing honest employee evaluations, consider providing a group evaluation with family members to coach them on your views of how they can piece together their strengths to ensure a peaceful and successful co-existence. This may include anointing one to lead. When two or more children are involved in the business, the possibility that you need to stay around a bit longer both as an active CEO/President or a visible chairman increases.

Ownership for How Many? Another rather tricky challenge is what to do with the ownership of the company when all the children are not involved. From purely an estate planning point of view, assuming you are paying your working child a salary, you continue to own 100% of the company. If you had two kids, eventually dividing the stock in 50% halves could raise some issues. One approach could be that you ensure your company bylaws allow for voting to handle all matters with a greater than 50% vote and then grant 51% to the working child and 49% to the other child. A couple of other points should be considered regarding this issue. First, the stock distribution issue can be avoided if you are able to arrange a sale to the working child where an earn-out provides for cash payments to you and your estate. If you have an earn-out, it is possible the non-working child's potential inheritance from your estate could be impacted by a failure on the part of the working sibling. Second, you all have to have an understanding of what, if any, additional value is being created anew by the working child. If the business is taking off and all is attributable to their new ideas and effort, a 50/50 split may not be a fair approach.

As you have more kids, this can present other challenges. Only one child would likely assume a future CEO role. If you have 34%—33%—33% splits, just like on the playground, eventually two gang up on one—even the person with 34%. This is an unfortunate scene if you live to see disputes of this nature play out and destroy the concept and value of what you have built. Coaching your children on the value of a Board to assume certain company decisions is one approach. Theoretically, even if there exists a bit of family jealousy, you would hope two of the three wouldn't vote for a value destroying initiative just out of spite. Practically speaking, it has happened. You can't expect, however, to resolve all of the issues that will pop up as you transition your business legacy to one or more of your children. The best you can do is provide an open, honest, fair and level playing field overlaid with rational intent.

KEY TAKEAWAYS

- If you have more than one child, questions arise as to how many you can take on or who should lead

- As difficult as it may be, you must assess each of your kids as you would any other teammate; do they have the skills to succeed in, and lead, your business

- For kids that do not want to be involved in the business, estate planning can fairly balance inheritance concerns

Memo #44
To: Dan
Re: Just a Phone Call Away

REGARDLESS OF YOUR METHOD OF OWNERSHIP TRANSITION, assuming you have maintained a solid familial relationship, you will likely be available as a chairman emeritus at any time. For the sake of maintaining those familial ties, however, try to make it when the involvement is invited. Nothing spoils a good family dinner like someone saying this is how we did it "in the good 'ole days" when "the good 'ole days" have been rendered a historical relic by your industry's evolving technology, products, service, customer base, etc.

Assuming you are no longer the owner, but having built or run the company yourself for a generation (or more), you will need some self-discipline to manage your own words when you inquire about the company. Be thoughtful about how your questioning can be perceived. That is, are you just chatting it up vs. your child viewing it as prying. It is their show now, they are making their own decisions. And some of those very likely will not be how you would have decided. If this agitates you, perhaps you shouldn't have left. You will, however, know you have engineered a successful transition if your child approaches you and asks for some "good 'ole fashioned advice!"

Where I do believe it is in Dan's and the company's best interest to uphold my legacy is around our vision and treatment of customers and vendors. High quality customer service will serve any company well and people's preference for fairness and transparency hasn't seemed to ever go out of style.

Depending upon your own child's work experience, if their only job has been within your company, they have known only one boss—night and day for their entire life! This can be a drawback if you are honest enough to admit you yourself don't have the perfect skillset across the board to hand down to a next generation. Staying honest, however, means coaching your child on the things you didn't feel you got right over the years. It can personally hurt a bit to fess up to shortcomings or failures, but learning from disappointment is as valuable as learning from a win. If you haven't chronicled all your wins and losses over the years, let your child know you are only a speed dial away and ready to share any recollections and experience that may help.

KEY TAKEAWAYS

- As you exit, agree upfront with your son or daughter on how you will and will not participate in the business going forward

- If you haven't chronicled your wins and losses over the years to share as examples, make sure your child knows you are only a phone call away

- If you have exited the business financially, be careful to consider yourself as an advisor now, not President

Memo #45
To: Dan
Re: External Training—
for Any Leader

UP TO THIS MEMO, the entire File #8 on succession cautioned the topics were those that a new entrepreneur was not likely to have top-of-mind in the early years. Let's get back to the mindset of a consideration worthy of every business at every stage of its life.

Not every person that starts a business carries a college degree in business. In fact, there are a few very famous college dropouts with multi-billion dollar-valued businesses—i.e. Gates, Zuckerberg, et. al. The point is, whether or not you or your child specifically studied business in college, the ability to start a business from the ground up or step into a business and learn it from a committed mentor/parent is a huge educational undertaking. There may be some specific skillsets that could be enhanced with some outside education such as accounting. There are others, however, such as being an effective salesperson, a respectable manager and a decisive leader that are many times best developed on the job within the learning lab that is the business.

Recommended Coursework. Even for business school curriculums, a great required course to add would be a psychology course. Many take it as an elective, however, if someone steers clear of that option, they miss out on understanding some of the core foundations of employer/employee or employee/customer relationships. Interpreting and understanding how or why somebody thinks a certain way can be beneficial when evaluating an employee for advancement opportunities or added responsibilities. An appreciation of their motivations can enable you to tailor roles that both get the best out of each individual but also provide the employee a positive and challenging working experience. That becomes a win-win for company and employee.

On the customer side of the equation, understanding personal motivations are a virtual requirement. Consider an insurance agent or financial planner. They must understand a customer's risk tolerance of potentially volatile capital markets not only at the moment of a transaction, but also how that evolves over one's lifespan. Understanding their background, history and family can better enable a connection of trust that can build a beneficial relationship.

Most college graduates complete a communication class that includes various forms of public speaking. Many business classes also include projects requiring teams to make presentations to the class. The ability to cogently organize and present one's ideas is paramount. As mentioned earlier, the number one sales job everyone needs to perfect is the ability to sell themselves. You just have to be comfortable getting up in front of individuals, small groups and sometimes the room to communicate a message that moves you and your company toward its goals.

One can think that life in a small business means never having to bother with such an undertaking and that mastering a staff meeting is all it will take. Think, however, of the ability to connect at a sales convention or industry trade show. If you want opportunities to publicize your company and help it grow, you may wish to join a trade association and undertake a leadership role. This engagement would likely entail being a part of meetings and committees where you will need to articulate and present your messages.

Mind These Gaps. If you or your child were not business school students and you haven't worked in any other companies previously, a potential blind spot develops. For your child, their sole observation of a management style is you. Further, they may have a difficult time separating your parenting approach from your management style.

Working in various jobs or in a larger company, one has the opportunity to work for a variety of people each with their own approaches to solving and addressing issues and problems. Learning from only one person is a distinct disadvantage and something to consider as you think about external training requirements.

Another worthy topic that isn't handled well in college is the ability to understand your own unconscious bias. I have some friends in larger companies and they have indicated this has become a rather popular training session. Of course, a small business does not have a budget necessarily to bring a teaching organization in for the day. Finding an opportunity to join some external seminar can provide you or your child an understanding of the pitfalls some people encounter when they are not aware of how their own attitudes and actions can impact various groups. It is not just age, race, religion or sex anymore. And even if you say you can look beyond those factors, what are the stereotypes you have heard and the perceptions you have developed over time that define each of those classes and how might those unconsciously affect your behavior and spoken word? Discrimination, intentional or not, is wrong. It can turn an otherwise fluidly operating team against itself and quickly impact your company's ability to deliver for the customer. To that matter, it is not just an internal company matter. If someone exhibits bias toward customers, vendors, etc., you will soon find out your company reputation has been irreparably damaged.

KEY TAKEAWAYS

- Certain skills you may lack require outside education, such as basic accounting

- Almost any job requires some selling skills; understanding basic psychology is a major plus

- Communication through clear, organized thoughts facilitates business connections

- If one is not aware of their unconscious bias, they might limit their ability to effectively connect more broadly

Leaving the Office at the Office

Memo #46

To: Dan

Re: Plan For, and Commit To, Time Away

THERE ARE SOME JOBS THAT READILY ALLOW a person to leave their work at the office. Think about an assembly line worker, a coal miner, etc. Maybe you walk away with some internal angst created by a foreman, but you can't put the work in your briefcase and take it home to the kitchen table. Granted, the executives at a manufacturing or mining facility may not be able to put tools down or walk away from the coal face so readily, but the rank and file do have that ability.

There are other businesses that create real challenges to managing your time, particularly those within a one-person start-up or those driven by the uncontrollable decisions or actions of others. For example, supplying and fitting medical care braces and products is dictated by the unfortunate and unplanned incidents of others. Accidents don't know 9 a.m. to 5 p.m. work schedules. A lawyer may have a client that decides to enter into a business contract right when your child's band concert is set to begin. Further, consulting and legal professionals are typically paid by the hour and require exactly that—hours!

When you own your own small business, like any other company, your success is going to be defined by what you do tomorrow. How does one know how to shut it off so family tranquility, to say nothing about recreation or sleep, can find its way into your life?

When I was a kid, there were some periods I could go a couple of days without seeing my Dad despite the fact he did not travel as a high school teacher. He worked hard, he coached hard and he played hard. On our vacations, which always included 24-hour driving trips to Florida at Spring Break and camping trips across the U.S. during August, Dad was all in. We loved those experiences and they helped define us as a family. Knowing the responsibilities of a small business owner can't be shelved for a week or two, preparation was critical to providing my family similar experiences and companionship.

Building a team you can trust, training them well and committing to coordinated planning should enable most small business owners to work around many conflicts. You may not clear them all, but that is part of the sacrifice of owning your own company. The key is not falling prey to allowing the business to dictate your entire personal life.

KEY TAKEAWAYS

- Prepare, prepare, prepare—and then you should be able to take time away with family

- A well-coached team attuned to the strategic initiatives and schooled in daily procedures will greatly facilitate the ability to take time off

TIME AND AGAIN, WHEN I LOOK AT PEOPLE that were successful through their college years, they also were highly engaged in other activities beyond the classroom. Whether it is athletics, as in my case, or the arts, or student government or a job to pay the bills, those students that were engaged outside the classroom seem to have learned more life lessons than those simply focused on the books. For me, swimming was about setting priorities, establishing routines, maintaining discipline and making sacrifices. It wasn't easy for me as I admitted early on, but I did get there in the end. Not bad for someone that seriously considered not traveling the college route.

In my business, once we re-launched Court Products, I prioritized what needed to get done and by when. The customer was the core of this thought process. I was able to figure out how much time each task might require which then allowed me to create a weekly schedule and develop a routine. From there, it was about being disciplined to stay on task in order to keep up with just the normal business requirements. Yes, there were some exceptions that popped up now and then, but having developed the routine ensured we weren't missing anything that could fall through the cracks and hurt the business. Getting a routine established helped me to know when I might be able to take that afternoon off for a family event or to get away for a round of golf with a vendor. The discipline of sticking to a routine provided confidence that we were getting things done right for the customer. Following our progress through to positive financial results also proved we were getting it done right for our team. Sacrifices were necessary along the way. If something didn't get done during the week, that weekend round of golf or tennis match got postponed. Even a fun mid-week outing with a vendor might have to take back seat to a customer's special project request. Sacrifices are, and will be, necessary.

In the early days, my failsafe catch-up approach was to go into the office very early in the mornings. Having been a swimmer, I was used to a fast start to the day. While I did have to skip my morning work-out to get caught up on these occasions, mornings hopefully find you refreshed after a decent night's sleep. In addition, assuming your business doesn't operate in shifts, you arrive much earlier than your team and the accompanying inbound phone calls from customers. Even if you are a manufacturing facility maximizing the efficiency of plant investment by running multiple shifts, you may be able to enjoy the relative quiet of the "front office." This was my approach to minimize interruptions and distractions and I often felt I could get twice the work done in the same amount of time had it been a regular business hour.

We've all been asked the question of whether we are a morning person or a night owl. Flipping the script on my preferred approach, I found hanging around late wasn't as productive because I had just been through a full day and frankly was often getting rather tired or hungry by evening hours. Time with the kids also always seemed more available at day's end than the hectic before-school rush. There are always likely to be some items that may pull you in at day's end given your customers or vendors may not be in the same time zone or even on the same "shift." Point is, when you need time to swim back to the surface, you need to figure out how you can be most productive and most effective. It is a personal preference with many variables, but you have to have the discipline to keep your business on track.

Finally, while we may live in the age of office cubicles, if you do have a door, you shouldn't feel bad about letting the team know you require some uninterrupted time. I would let the team know that something required my undivided attention and I didn't want to be interrupted for an hour or two. (And for the cynics, it wasn't a nap!)

KEY TAKEAWAYS

- Recount the traits that drove you to start the business, they are likely the same that will provide confidence to be successful and take time off

- Explore approaches to gaining "me time" in order to catch up on, or get ahead of, the daily grind

Memo #48
To: Dan
Re: Healthy Body,
Healthy Perspective

YOU HAVE PROBABLY SEEN YOUR SHARE of those articles about "being your own boss." And yes, owning and operating your own business does allow one the luxury to make the call on how much time to dedicate to the business. Being an absentee business owner, however, just may provoke consequences that you can't fix in enough time to prevent lasting damage to your company. Should a quality problem develop and get into the marketplace or a team culture develop that parodies "if he doesn't care, we don't care," you may have irreparably destroyed your business' value.

Harry S. Truman, the 33rd President of the United States, had a plaque on his desk reading "the buck stops here." The statement was derived from the old saying that people liked to pass the buck, or pass the responsibility. As a small business owner, the buck absolutely stops with you! Taken in total, of course, you cannot execute all the tasks and responsibilities to execute your company's daily operations. But you will need to manage them: 24/7/365.

To do this, one of the responses at the top of my list I mention to people that ask the question "what does it take to run your own business?" is maintain a commitment to yourself to stay in good physical condition. It is imperative in order to handle the relentless pace of activity necessary to run a successful business. People deal with stress in different ways and that stress can take a difficult toll on your physical well-being. If you have a family, your collective livelihood is tied to the business. You owe it to them, as well.

The increasing popularity of 24/7 health clubs offers you an opportunity to gain access to meaningful exercise options early, late, weekends and any other time for which you can't make up another excuse. Instill that discipline and make it happen. I can tell when my energy and focus is not where it needs to be. Over the years, I believe some of our best accomplishments were occurring during periods when I was dedicated to personally engaging in varied physical activities including gyms, pools, tennis courts, etc. Hard morning workouts provide a refreshed sense of being ready to handle the next set of challenges. During the kids' school-age years, they were pre-occupied with getting to school, so mornings at home were hectic. Thus, I committed to using that time for maintaining my healthy life style and getting an early start at work. Evenings, though, provided opportunity for family dinners, helping out with homework and even bedtime stories in the early years. It was easier for me to fit in the natural flow, to be helpful and to be present.

There may be some of you that enjoy a weekly tee-off time with friends, or a weekday tennis, soccer or hockey time slot at night. That is OK, of course. The goal is to take some time for yourself and unwind while also enjoying some physical activity.

If you need some time at home to think through business matters, there are also more mundane activities you can use to stay active and provide yourself some time to think. For me, I could always "get away" when I was cutting the grass. It's not like anyone can talk to you. On a number of occasions, I have solved various business-related issues or thought through some potential new ideas while powering back and forth in a Zen-like trance to the drone of the mower. It is actually relaxing in an odd way. There are no interruptions, it's a bit therapeutic and occurs on a regular basis. Add to that, I am not really stealing time from anything else. You may be thinking I'm obsessive, but it is really about compartmentalizing your attention to the business during periods where you are not stealing time away from family and friends.

KEY TAKEAWAYS

- Though you can't do it all, you are responsible; figure out your best way to handle the stress

- A start-up business needs its visionary; commit to stay in good physical condition

- Consider some of your mundane daily tasks as opportunities to complete some private thinking

Memo #49
To: Dan
Re: Everyone Needs a Vacation

BELIEVE IT OR NOT, I GOT MY FIRST SMARTPHONE IN 2016—yeah, plenty of people have marveled at my ability to hold off on this "fad!" As I look back, maybe it was a blessing in disguise. I didn't have 24-hour access on vacations so I had no choice but to unplug and trust in the team. I hope, upon reflection, the team saw it as my vote of confidence in their collective abilities. Not that it influenced me, but I always got a bit of a chuckle how my father-in-law would always call me from his vacations at about 4:55 p.m. on a Friday. I was never sure if he was aware of this timing or if he was actually checking in on me to see if I was actually gutting out the whole week. I have never replicated that approach because I didn't want my team to feel the way I had. It is not about checking up, it's about checking in—a big difference.

Arranging time to attend a special event or take a vacation requires some smart planning within a small business. Are you going to deny a teammate's attendance to a family wedding just because it is peak season—of course not. The composition of your team may impact everyone's ability to target their first-choice days off. If you have some older teammates, their kids may be grown so they are not tied to typical school vacation schedules. Similarly, you may have some younger teammates that either have very young children or don't yet have families of their own. In the early years, however, we seemed to have a team that was all on a school-dominated calendar. There were some trips my family planned where I joined late or returned early to ensure appropriate resources at the company. As a new company, I didn't feel our total pay and benefits were quite at market, so I felt this was one way to give the team something extra. It is just one of the sacrifices a small business owner must be prepared to make. Pulling a "I'm the boss" trump card on something like this would guarantee a morale death spiral.

On my family's vacations, particularly as my kids grew a bit older, we did engage in one collective work-related activity. I was always on the lookout for new and creative apparel that might make sense for our customers. It was also helpful to check out design trends and creative approaches being expressed on new apparel that we could adapt to our not-for-profit clubs and organizations. And, something not to be overlooked in my particular business, my kids would also help me identify the contemporary trends appealing to their generation. Wherever we were, we would check out the local t-shirt shops looking for inspiration. We would even turn the search into a friendly competition within the family to see who could find the "coolest" shirt in the shop. Not stopping there, I challenged them to think about how they could adapt the design to suit our customers. Of course, my wallet was often a tad lighter after these excursions and the kids really seemed to look forward to them. Bottom line, it really did serve to further the business while also having some creative fun with the family! It also served a nice way to talk to my kids about the company, what we do and how we continually strive for success.

There are many larger companies that offer tours of their operations. It is not that you can spy on a competitor, rather you might learn some ideas for your business by looking at other operational business models. Your family might also enjoy learning how "stuff is made!"

As you bring on new hires, they should understand when your busy and peak operational periods hit the calendar. It is worth a question to screen during your hiring process. If you are a Main Street retailer and are focused on a strong Christmas selling season, you can't afford to have people taking multiple days off just before December 25th. Reading your own business flow can also allow you to adapt your ability to provide vacation days. Many pre—and post-national holiday time periods can slow down for some businesses. Fridays post-Thanksgiving are notoriously slow outside retail. Is it easy to grant that as an additional benefit? I also bundled Memorial Day, Fourth of July and Labor Day and offered each of the three team-mates working for me the opportunity to add one day to one of those summer holiday weekends. They were able to work it out without any strife and keep track over the years to keep it balanced and fair. Likewise at Christmas, I allow the staff to split up by taking an extra day on the 24th or 26th.

When you are young and very eager to prove yourself you tend to drive non-stop and may not realize the effect you are having on your-self at the time or later down the road. You don't want to burn your-self out. As the old saying goes, life is a marathon, not a sprint. Your vacation habits are likely to influence your teammates. If you don't take it, they may feel it will reflect negatively upon them when they take vacation time to enjoy a well-earned battery re-charging. This can build up into negative team morale which could inflict harm upon the business. Be a good role model.

Importantly, one of the drivers for training each of our teammates on all the different roles and responsibilities is to prepare for the day we need the resource coverage for sick days, vacations or even someone quitting. In our weekly meetings, reviewing the calendar is a routine item on the agenda. It enables us to plan ahead, cover open cus-tomer and administrative items or refresh someone on needed skills.

- Don't "check up" on the team from your vacation, "check in" on the business

- You deserve time away like everyone, but be prepared to sacrifice

- Explore ways to have fun with the family and complete business diligence; creatively check out how other companies operate, advertise, sell, etc.

- Explore creative ways to grant days off by taking advantage of seasonal "slow" days

Memo #50
To: Dan
Re: Work/Life Balance

WE BEGAN THIS BOOK BY TALKING ABOUT your own personality traits and whether those fit the small business lifestyle (Memo #4—Is Your Personality the Right Fit?). In any kind of company of any size, someone's obsessive work attitudes may drive to the fore and create a workaholic. The problem with these personalities is two-fold. First, they can drive people away with their relentless demands for time. And, second, they can drive themselves over the brink physically or mentally. In a larger company, replacing the impacted staff or individual may be a less disruptive issue in the broader scheme. In a small business, if that workaholic is the owner, then significant problems arise that can end up crippling the business.

My wife has always said that I don't really enjoy the extremes of anything—with the possible exception of ice cream! I trust her to help me ensure my priorities remain in balance and align with the family's. Obviously, as a small business owner, providing for your family means dedicating a great deal of effort to your work. The times when I did find it difficult to leave the office at the office mostly dealt around company personnel matters. Sometimes you need a sounding board or just the opportunity to talk out loud about a gnawing business issue to someone that you can trust. During those instances, my wife has always graciously allowed me to talk out my concerns during our evening walks around the neighborhood. Dan also has found that while he never remembers any specific incidents where I came home and totally vented, he now appreciates why I made time to work out or spend time in my workshop.

Probably one of my "appraisals" I value most is that my kids score me "very high" at being there when it mattered. They have known some classmates who have had some disappointments. Volleyball, swim meets, golf tourneys, little league, father/child camps, I was generally there. Maybe not at all the away events, but attending these types of activities is also a great way to get away from the daily grind and clear the mind. It reminds you that life is happening outside your company's doors.

As a distributor, we perform an annual count of our inventory. For a couple of days over the kids' Christmas breaks, I would have the kids come in and we would tackle the rather mundane task of counting the physical items within each box. While the kids may not have thought counting t-shirts was the highlight of their Winter break, they did get rewarded with an envelope holding a few bucks and we enjoyed the opportunity to share some pizza and get caught up. They gained a small amount of insight into the business and I gained resolution of the most tedious of tasks! In reality, I gained some Dad time with two people I treasure.

One note of caution is about the early years. This is the time when the business sinks or swims around your energy and input. It is also the time you develop your habits and form your company's culture. Thus, while easier said than done, with all the pressures upon you and all the new things to learn, you must take time to decompress by tending to your family, your health and your non-work friendships.

As Joe Maddon, manager of my 2016 World Series Champion Chicago Cubs, repeated throughout the championship season for a very young and developing team:

> *"Don't let the pressure exceed the pleasure."*

You don't need me to say "good luck!" By starting your own business, you have demonstrated initiative beyond that of most of your peers. But do have fun!

KEY TAKEAWAYS

- Know if you have "workaholic" tendencies; better yet, know how to manage them

- Life does happen outside the doors to your business, be a part of it

- Find fun ways to engage your kids in discussions about, or the work within, your business

"Afterword"

CELEBRATE YOUR SUCCESSES

I learned the painful truth about compounding interest the hard way. When we re-launched Court Products in 1990 and focused on the national not-for-profit clubs and organizations while liquidating the racquetball business, John and I came to an agreement on how much I would pay him for the 20% of the business I intended to run.

While he refused to bankroll the previous business any longer, John did agree to provide me "seller financing" for my plan. We drafted up a promissory note, complete with a fixed interest rate of 9%. I had my head down making that business work during the first four years. Nevertheless, I still had to borrow some additional money from John to build inventory for a growing customer base. Because of the focus on running the business, I hadn't really focused on keeping track of how the interest was accruing on that note. I think John had a better intuitive sense a year or two in that my plan was starting to move the company toward profitability and was, therefore, content to let me set the repayment schedule.

About five years in, I sat down with my accountants and told them I wanted to start to pay John back with all the interest. Boom, it hit me! That 9% interest rate along with the working capital financing had nearly doubled the outstanding principal value of the note I owed John. I then had a couple of years where I was able to just pay the accruing interest thereby holding the principle level. To this day, I distinctly remember a 1997 fall evening neighborhood walk with my wife when I said "I'm going to be working for your old man for life, and I mean life!" In fact, it is so burned in my memory that I can point out the exact square on the neighborhood sidewalk I was standing on when I said that to her!

It certainly isn't within my nature to throw up my hands, so I set about at least paying the newly accruing interest in addition to token amounts of principle. As we continued to commit our energies to the new company, thankfully success followed. I even began to make more modest payments to start whittling down the principle. About six years later, I started to believe there could be a light at the end of this debt tunnel. I even thought I might be able to pay it off a lot sooner than I initially anticipated. Before long, I began making occasional additional lump sum payments.

Outside of my relationships with my wife and two kids, my biggest accomplishment was now within reach. My wife and I invited John and my mother-in-law, Patty, out to dinner. I gave a toast thanking John for the tremendous opportunity he gave me to join Court Products in the first place. In addition, all his help, guidance and encouragement during the turnaround not only helped me along, but also formed a truly meaningful and special relationship. I then reached into my pocket and presented him with the last check that paid off his note in full. I was now the 100% owner of Court Products! What an incredible feeling—100% mine, no note to John, no note to a bank, no investors, no partners. It sounds selfish, but yes, it was all mine. To experience that feeling made the entire journey incredibly worthwhile.

I can only hope that you readers who decide to pursue your dream can one day experience that feeling. And when you do, celebrate the success!

Dan—anything here resonate?

Acknowledgements

This project began at our 2016 family Christmas gathering. Todd expressed a frustration at not memorializing his lessons learned over his business career, particularly as his son, Dan, was now becoming very engaged in the company. Taking the opportunity of a career sabbatical, Lynn offered to help organize and write the account.

Nearly a year later, both our wives, Kathy (Todd) and Kathleen (Lynn) Stetson, have provided incredibly positive support for this project. Their helpful early editing has also removed the "Stetson Brothers' Dialect" and made for a more professional read to a wider audience.

Fittingly, Danny Stetson designed the front cover. We asked him to capture what the book meant to him—complete with his Dad's own handwriting for the title.

Kevin Lawler, a Venture Capital and Angel investor familiar with small businesses and startup ventures, provided excellent real-world and insightful feedback.

Thank you also to our book cover editor and copy formatting designer, Jim Scattaregia, who has provided a catchy and clearly readable product.

We would also like to thank Fred Schroyer at My Next Season for his early guidance on what it takes to organize, write and sell a book. His early enthusiasm was a tremendous catalyst.

Finally, a special thank you to our editor, Karen Fox, who provided highly valuable advice on the presentation of our thoughts and ideas and provided strong encouragement to get the story out to those who could most benefit. All this positivity while cleaning up her home from Hurricane Harvey.

About the Authors

TODD STETSON has spent 30 years working at Court Products, first as an employee, then as an integral part of reshaping its path to eventually owning it. He has served on his community's park board as an elected official and as a member of the board of directors for a local community bank. Todd graduated from the University of Wyoming with a BS

in Marketing. He captained and assistant coached the UW Swimming Team. Todd and his wife, Kathy, have two children, Danny and Julie and one granddaughter from Danny and his wife Laura. Outside of his professional career, his passions are hiking and photographing wildlife in the mountains.

LYNN STETSON is a financial risk management executive with over 30 years of experience. He has functionally reported to the Board of Directors of two Dow 30 companies— Bank of America and GE Capital. He has held roles covering consumer, small business and global investment banking risk, including five years in London where his family enjoyed

living in and traveling throughout Europe, the Middle East and Africa. Lynn and his wife, Kathleen, have two children, Clare and Griffin. Lynn enjoys the discovery of learning from new people, new activities and new destinations. Like Todd, Lynn graduated from the University of Wyoming and captained the UW Swimming Team. He also earned an MBA at Indiana University.

For more on *Memos to Dan*, please visit: **memostodan.com**

96884837R00130

Made in the USA
Columbia, SC
04 June 2018